PEACOCK
AN ADULT COLORING BOOK

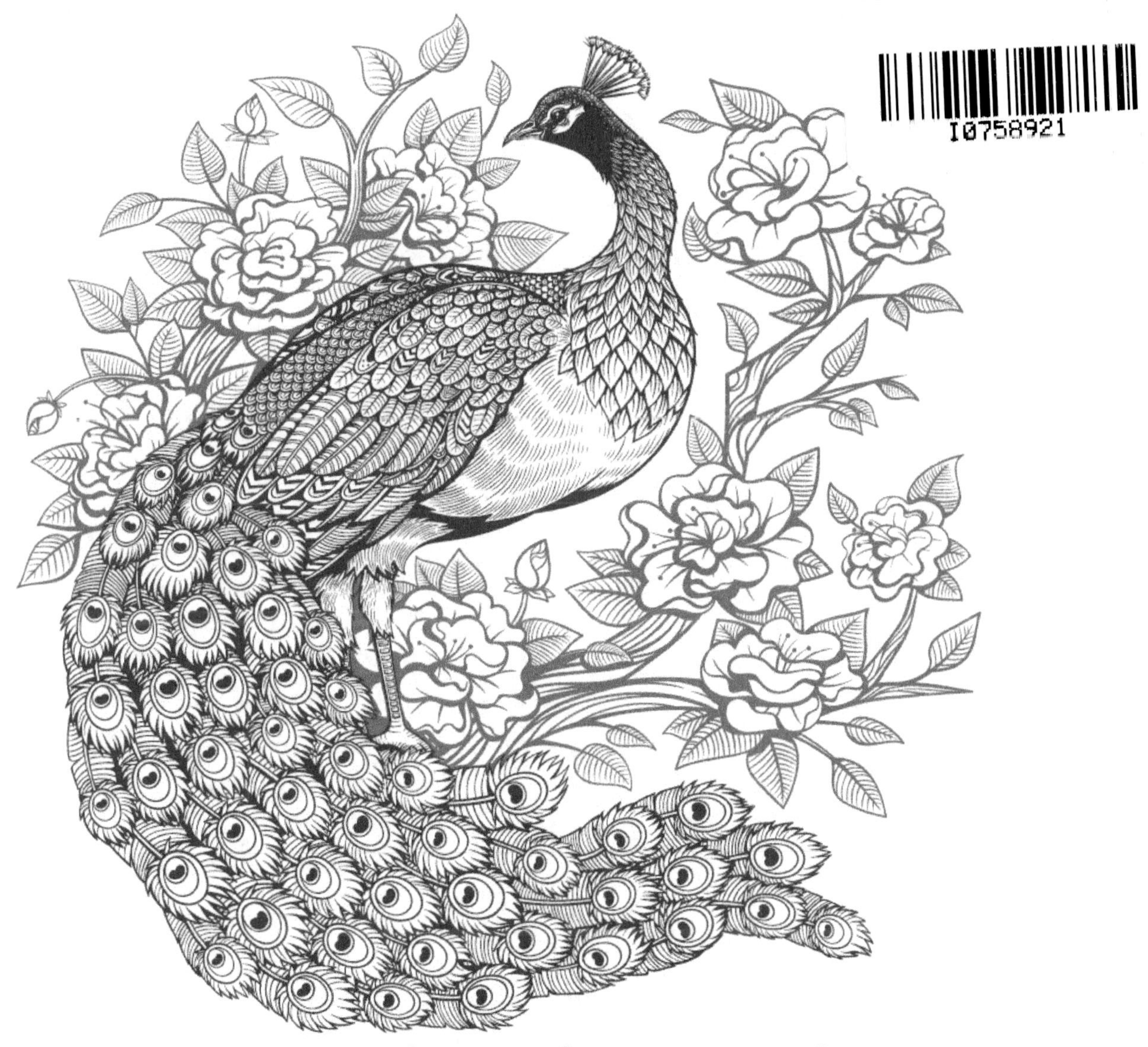

52 Peacock Coloring Pages

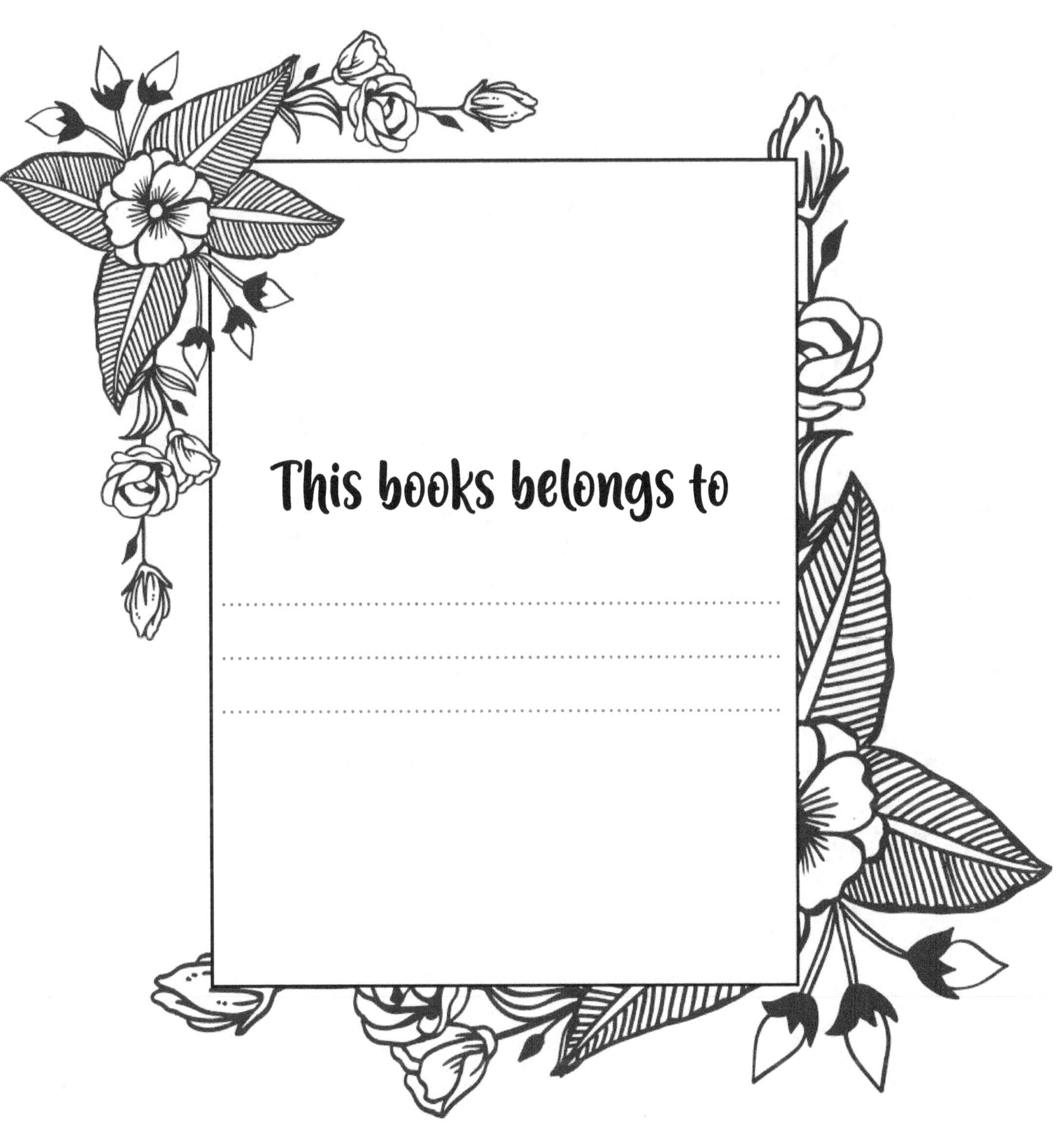
This books belongs to

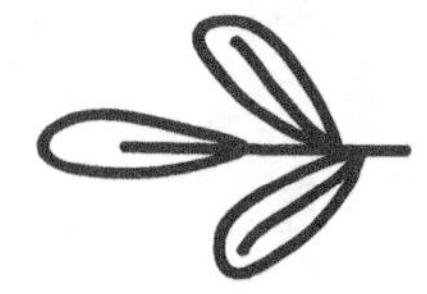 # Color Test Page 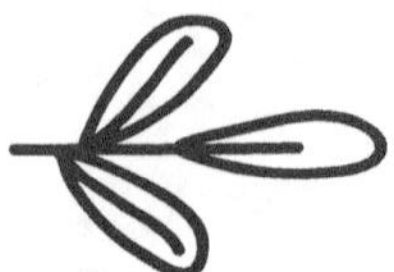

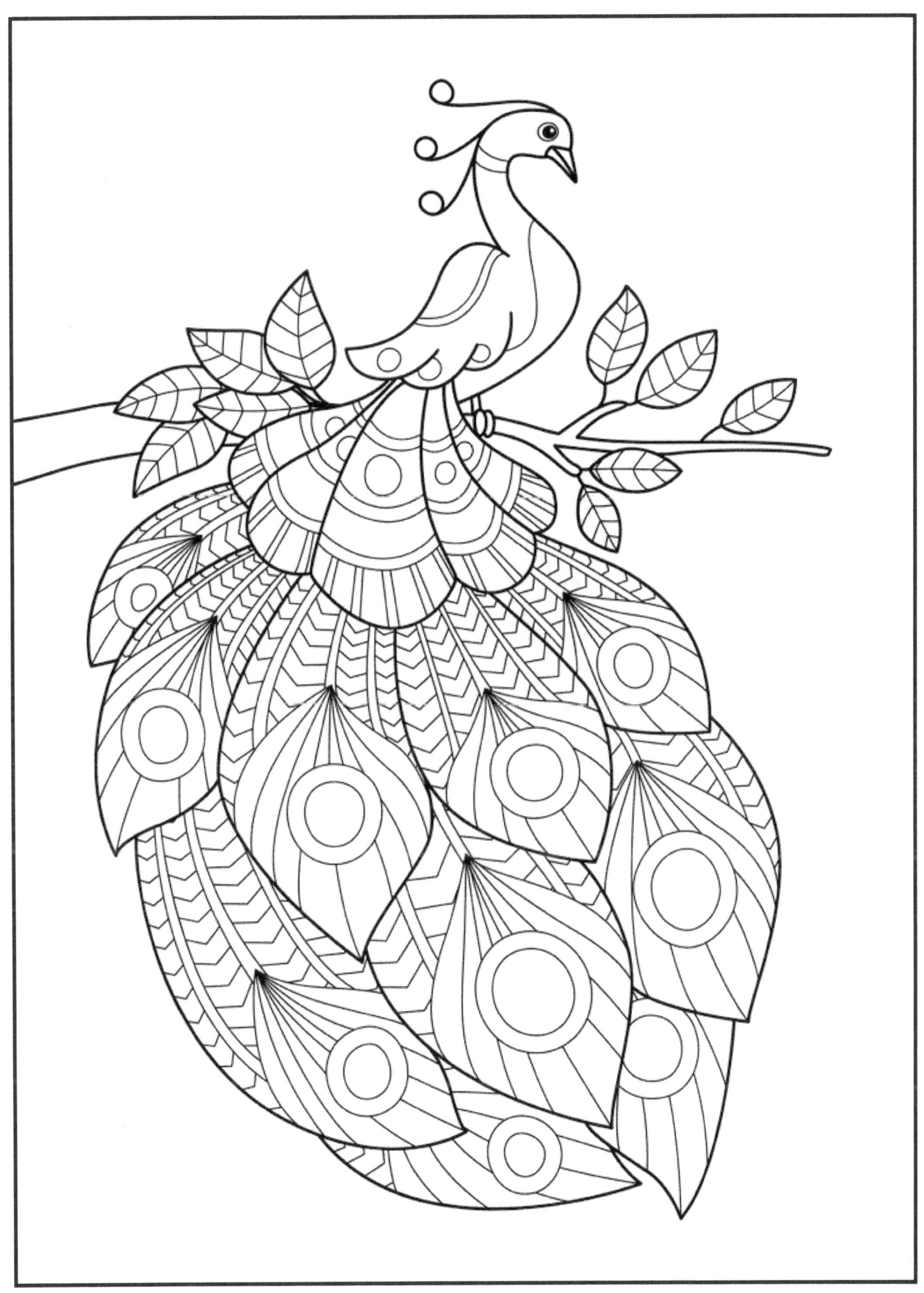

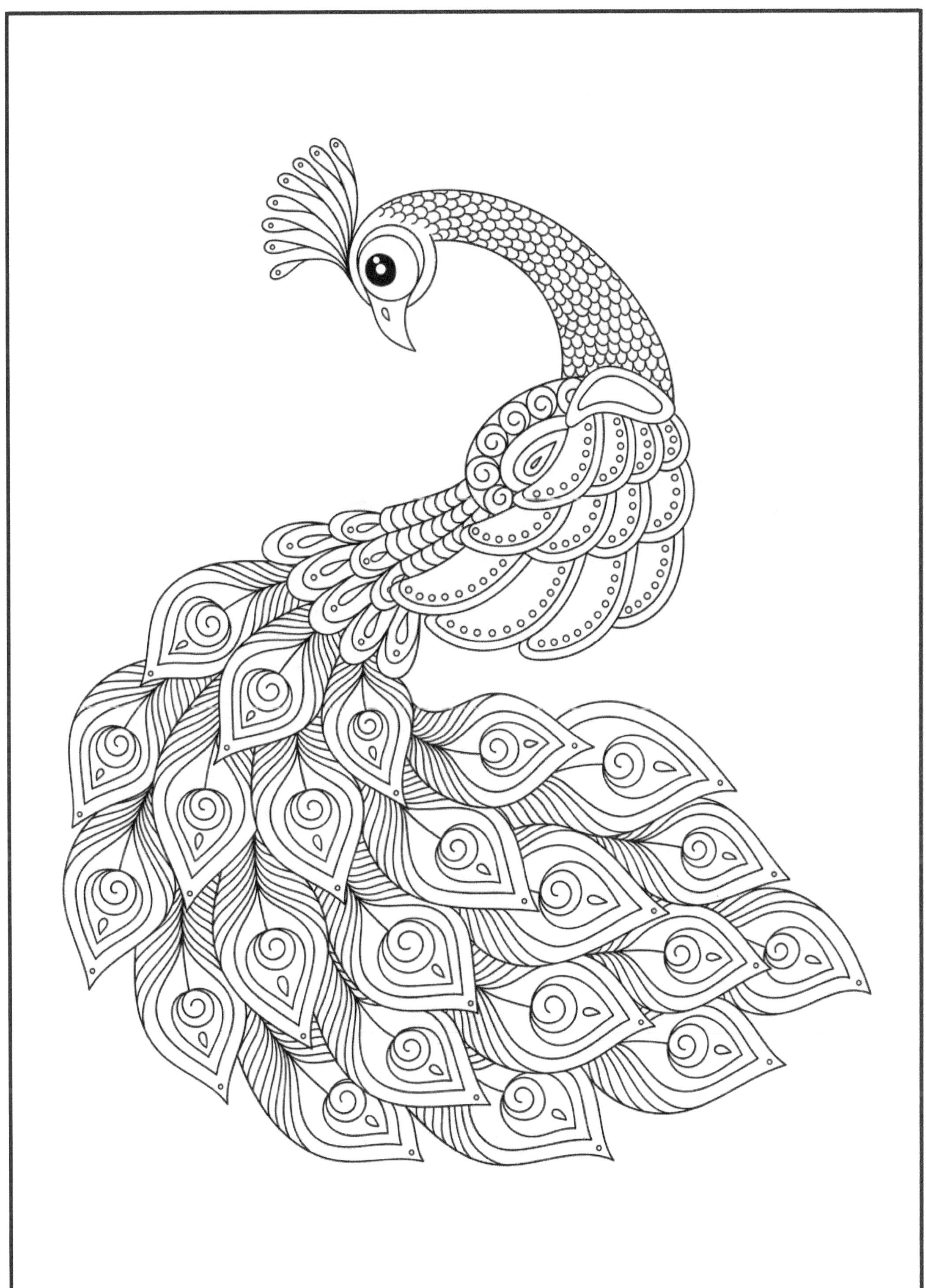

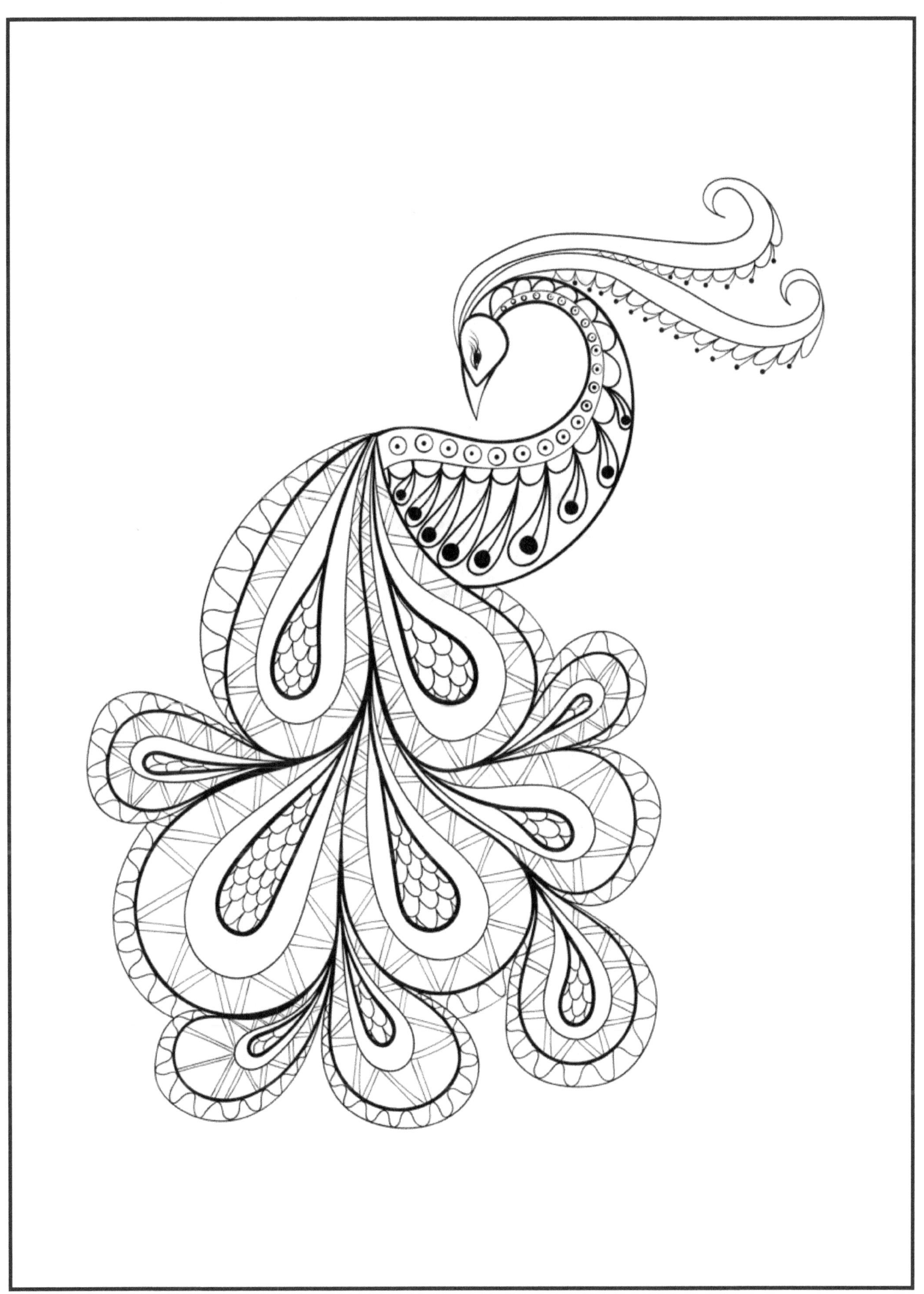

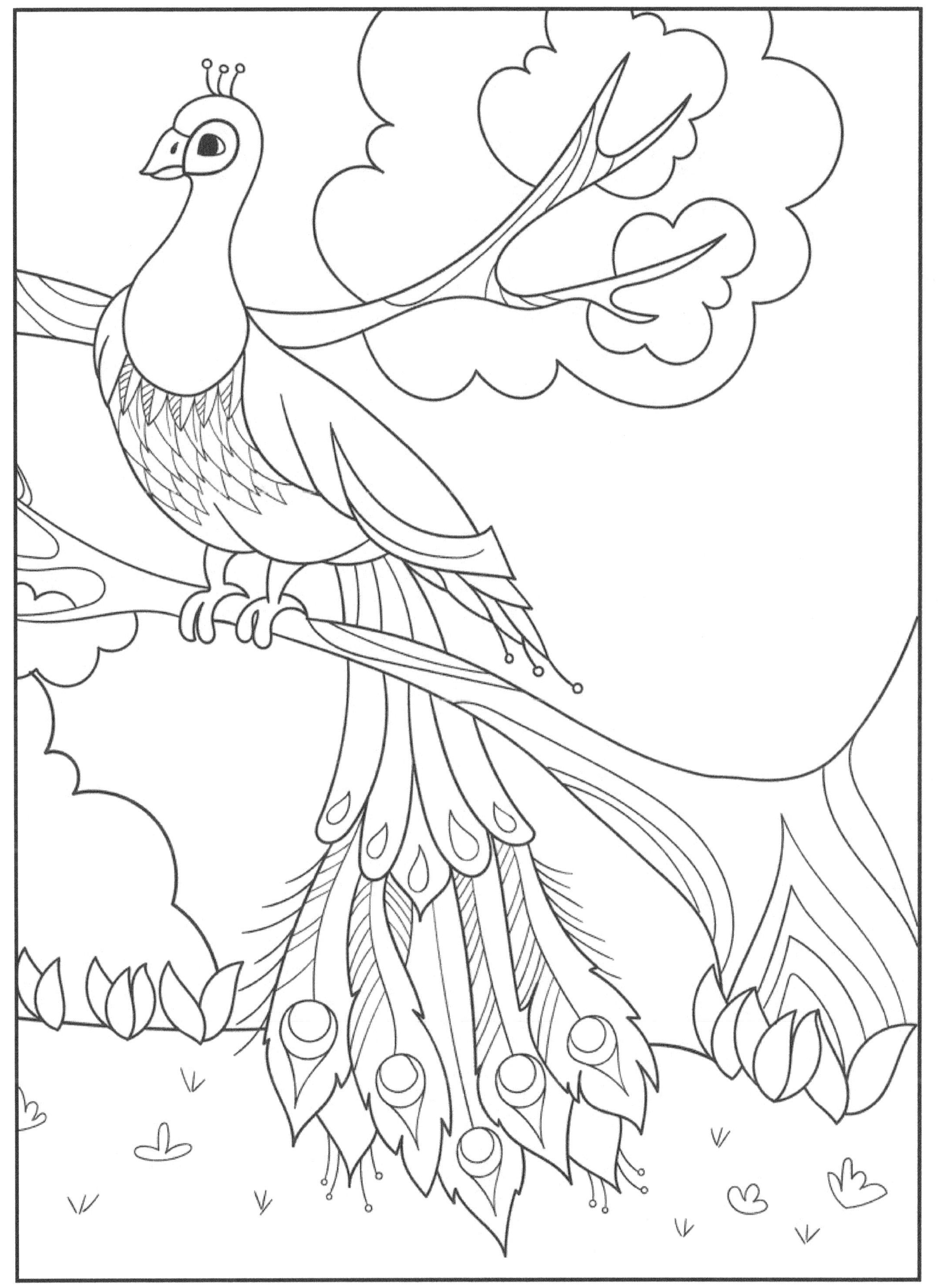

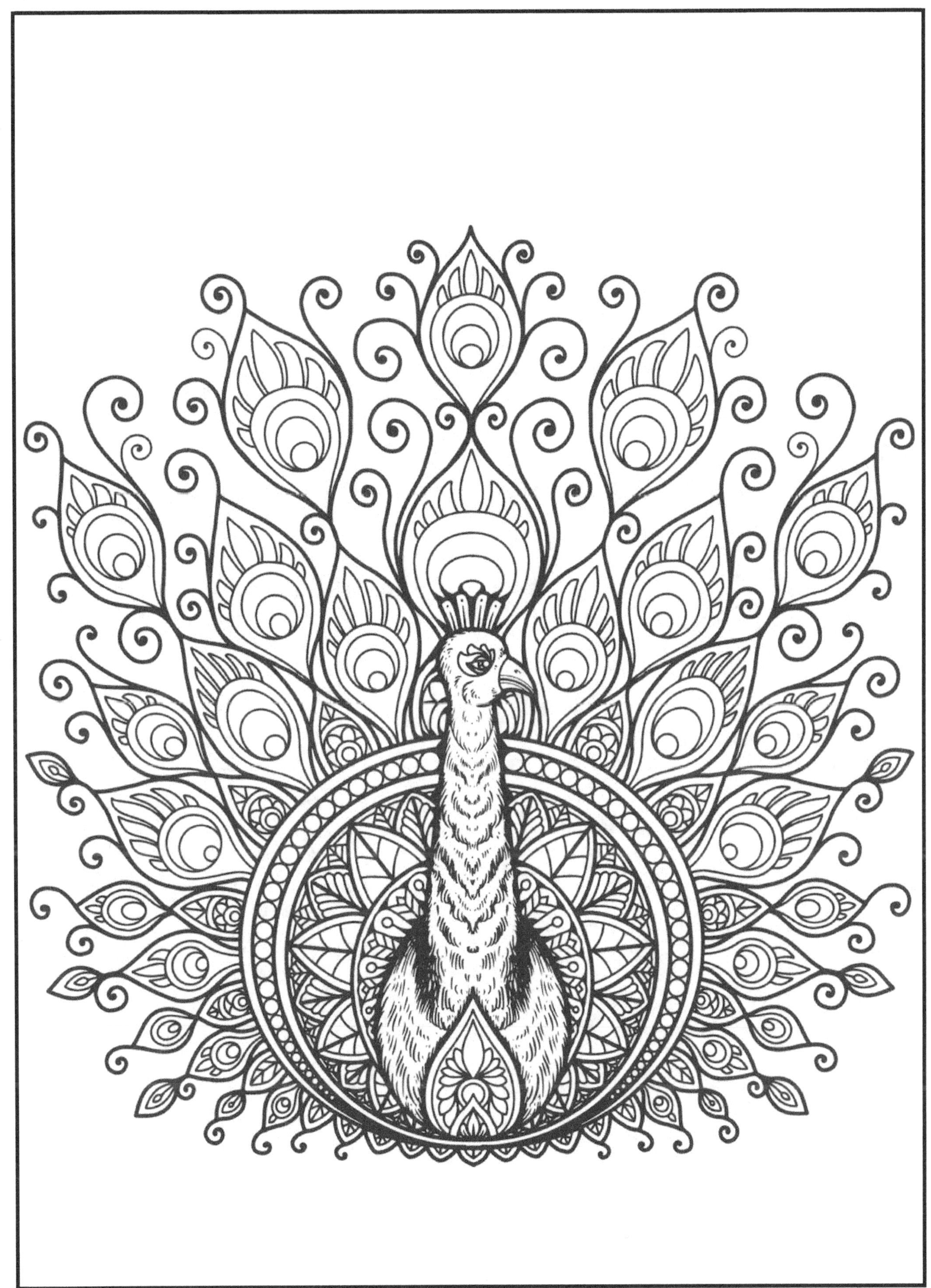

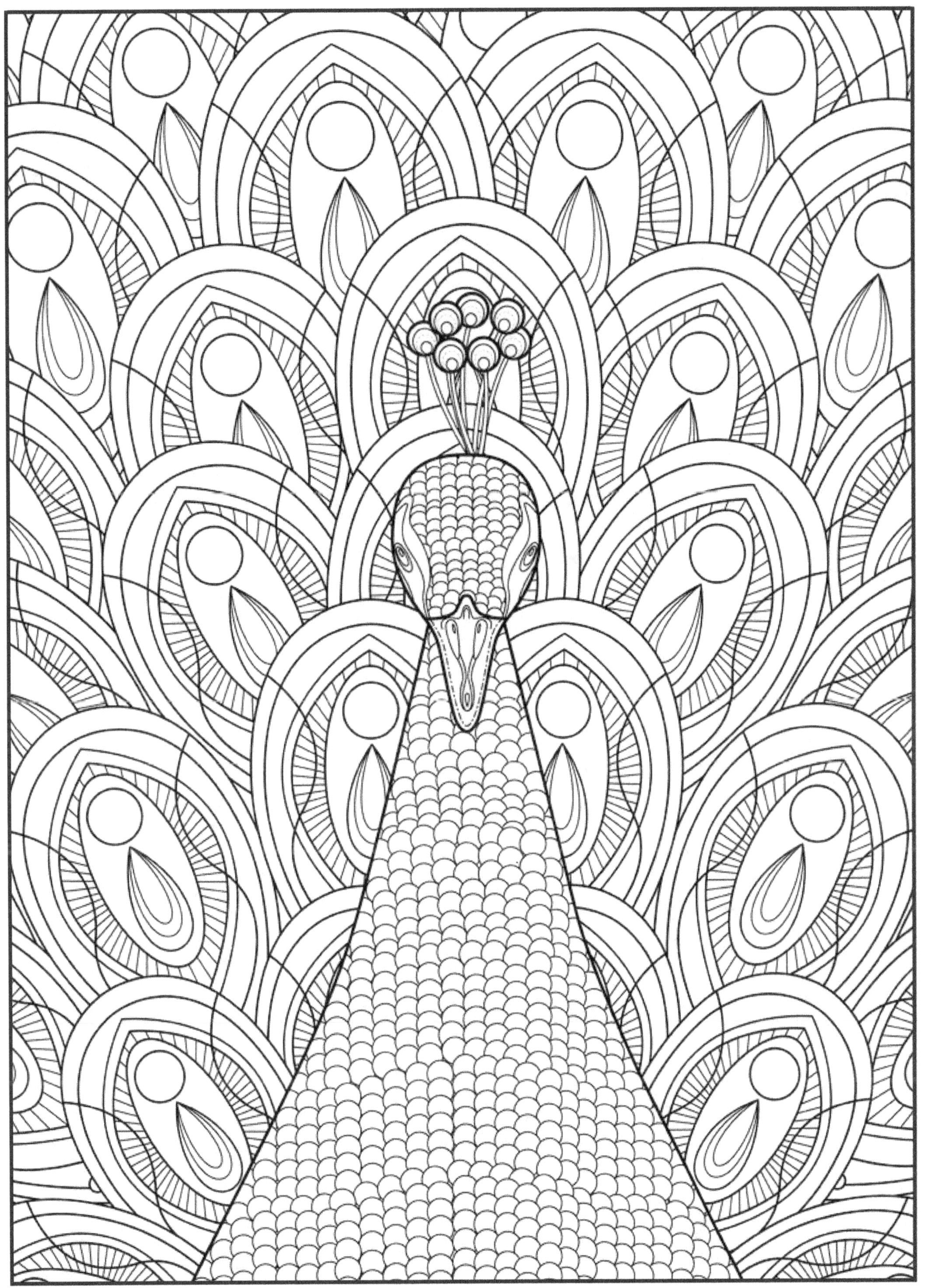

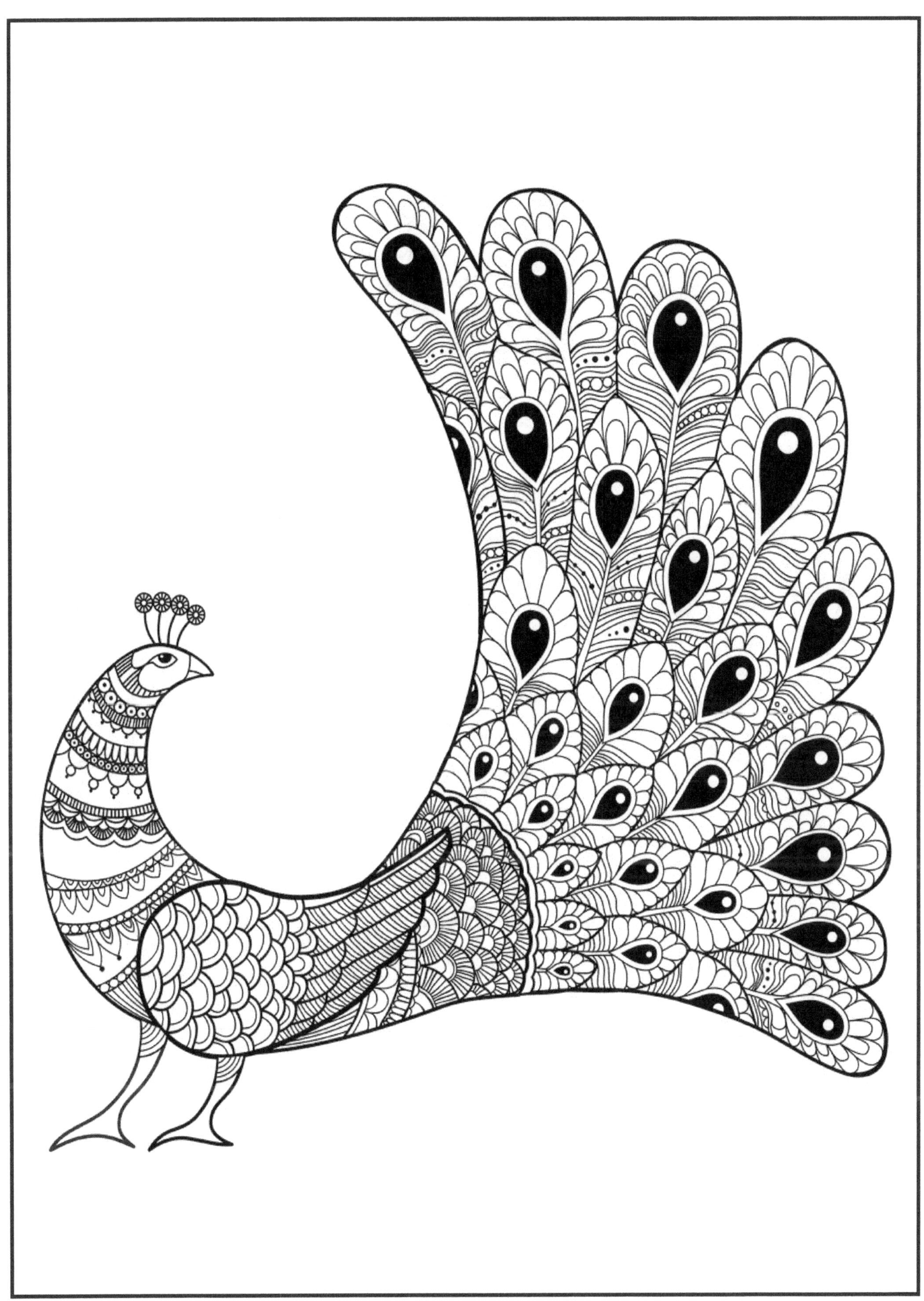

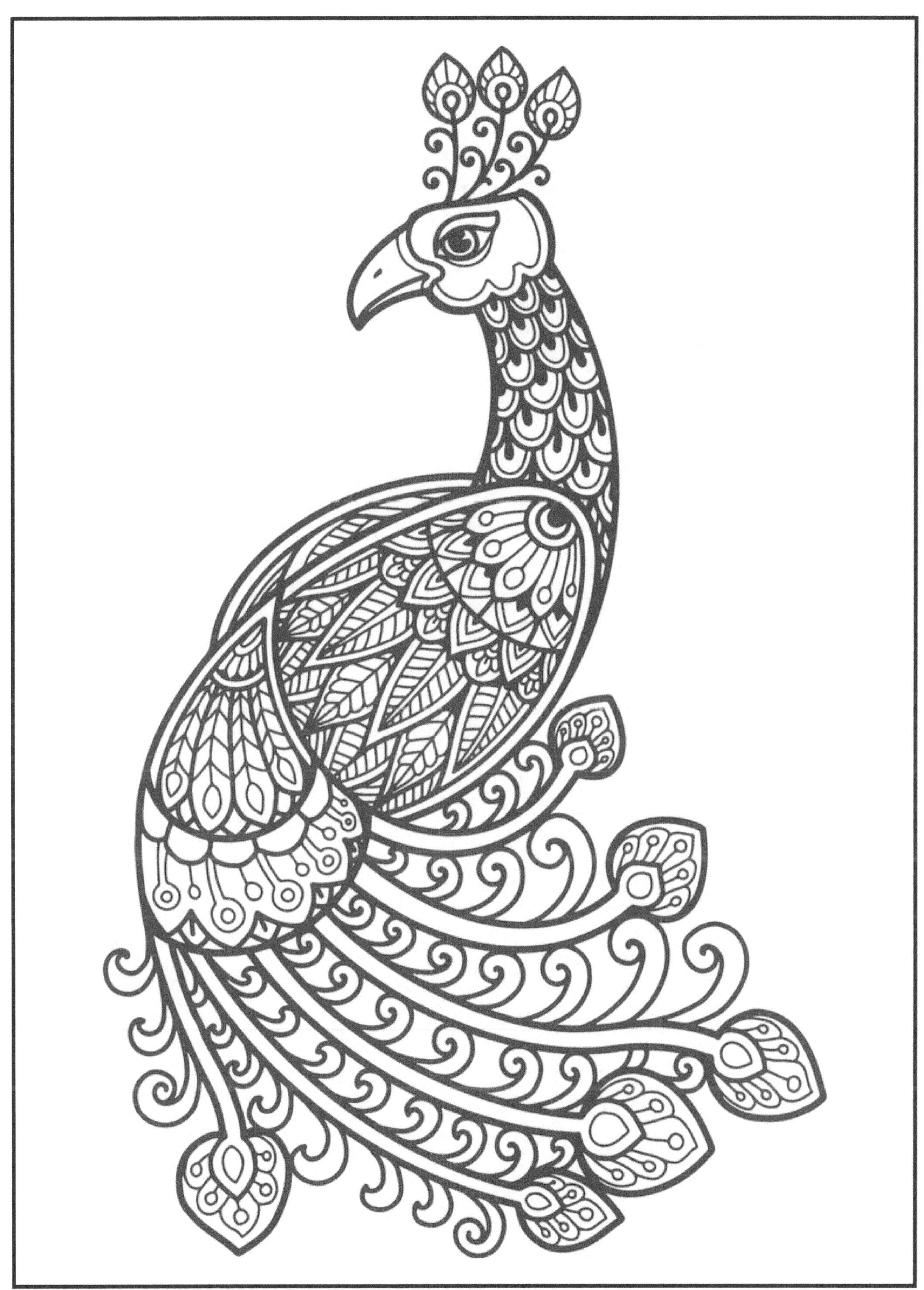

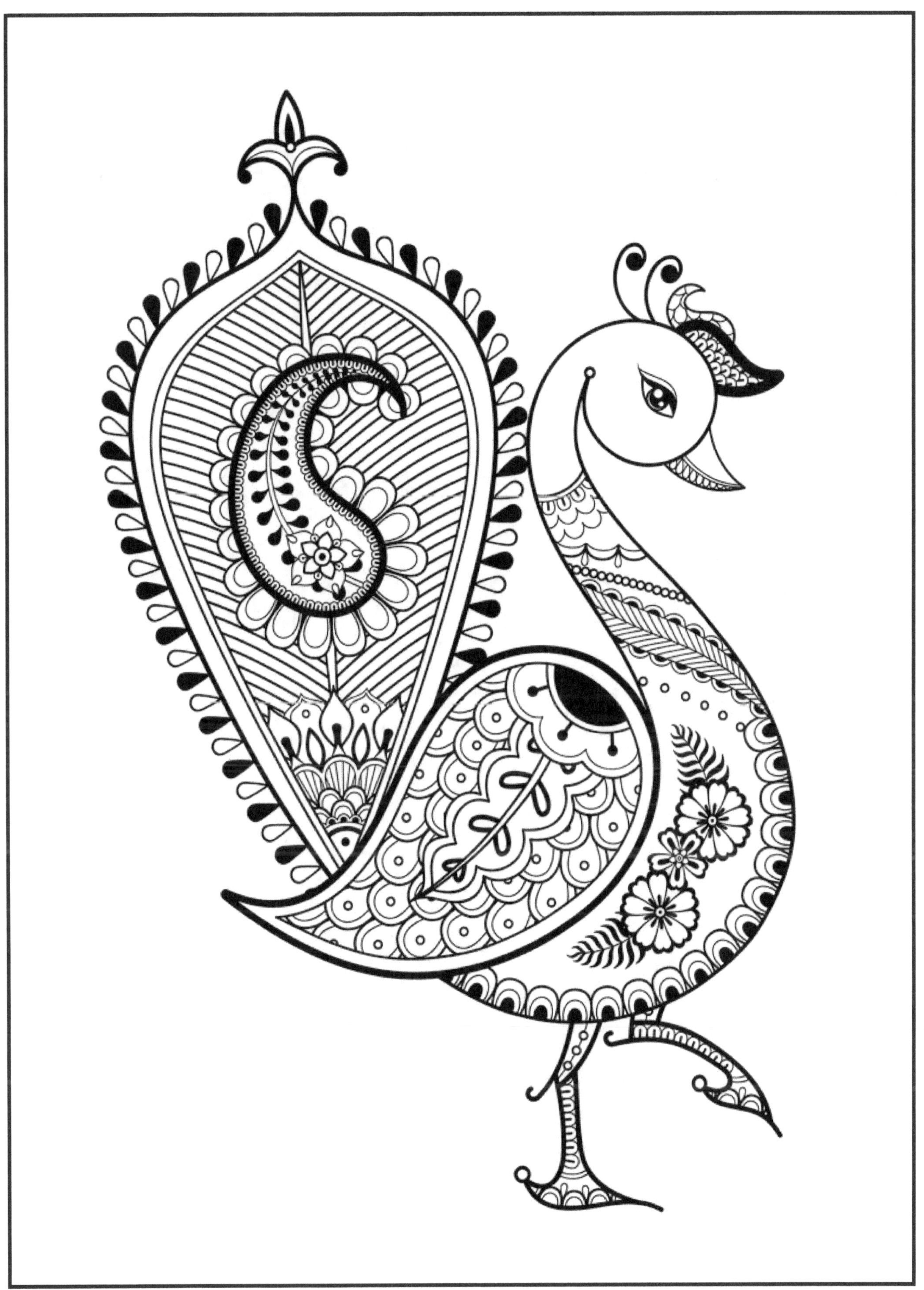

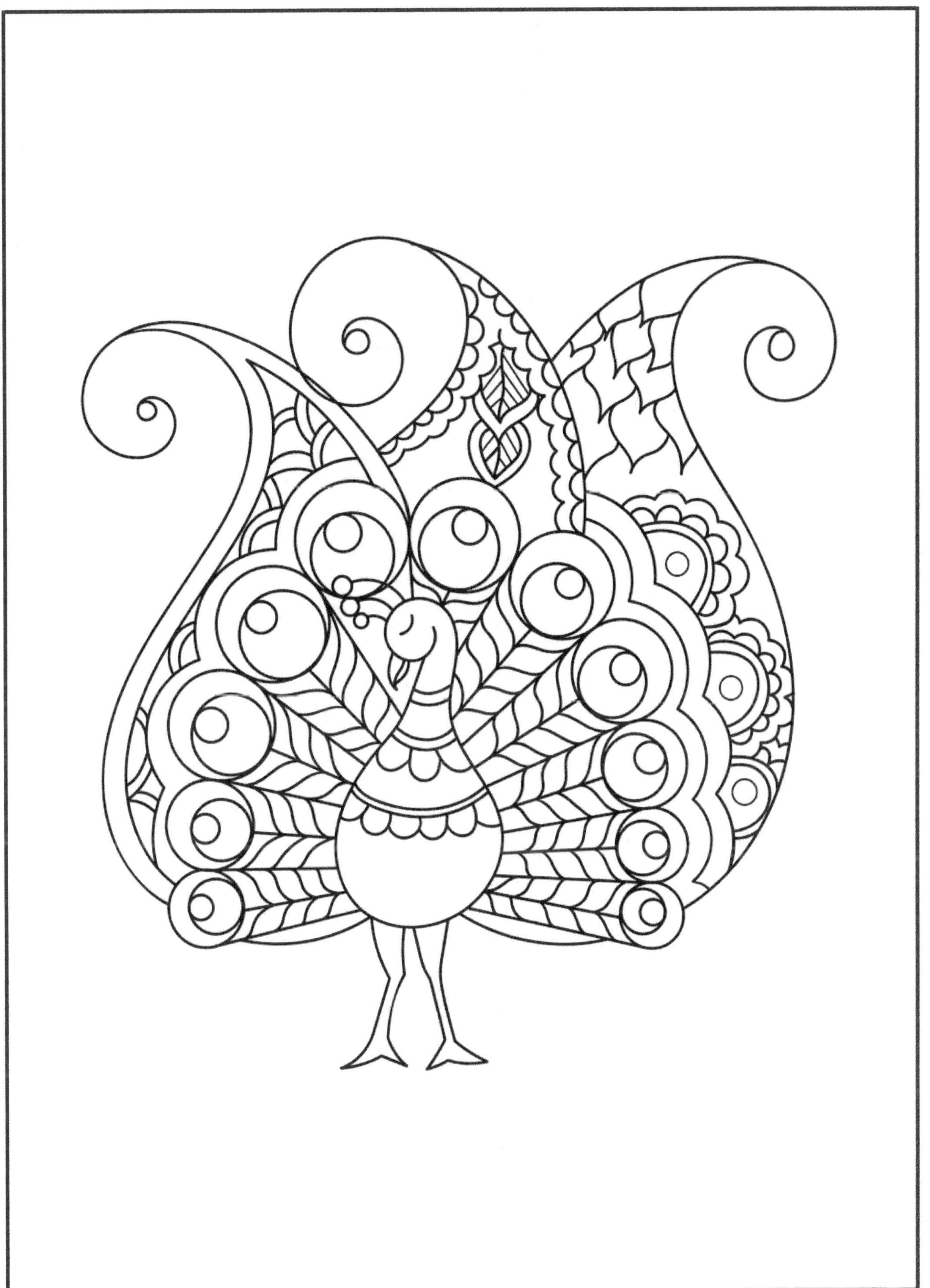

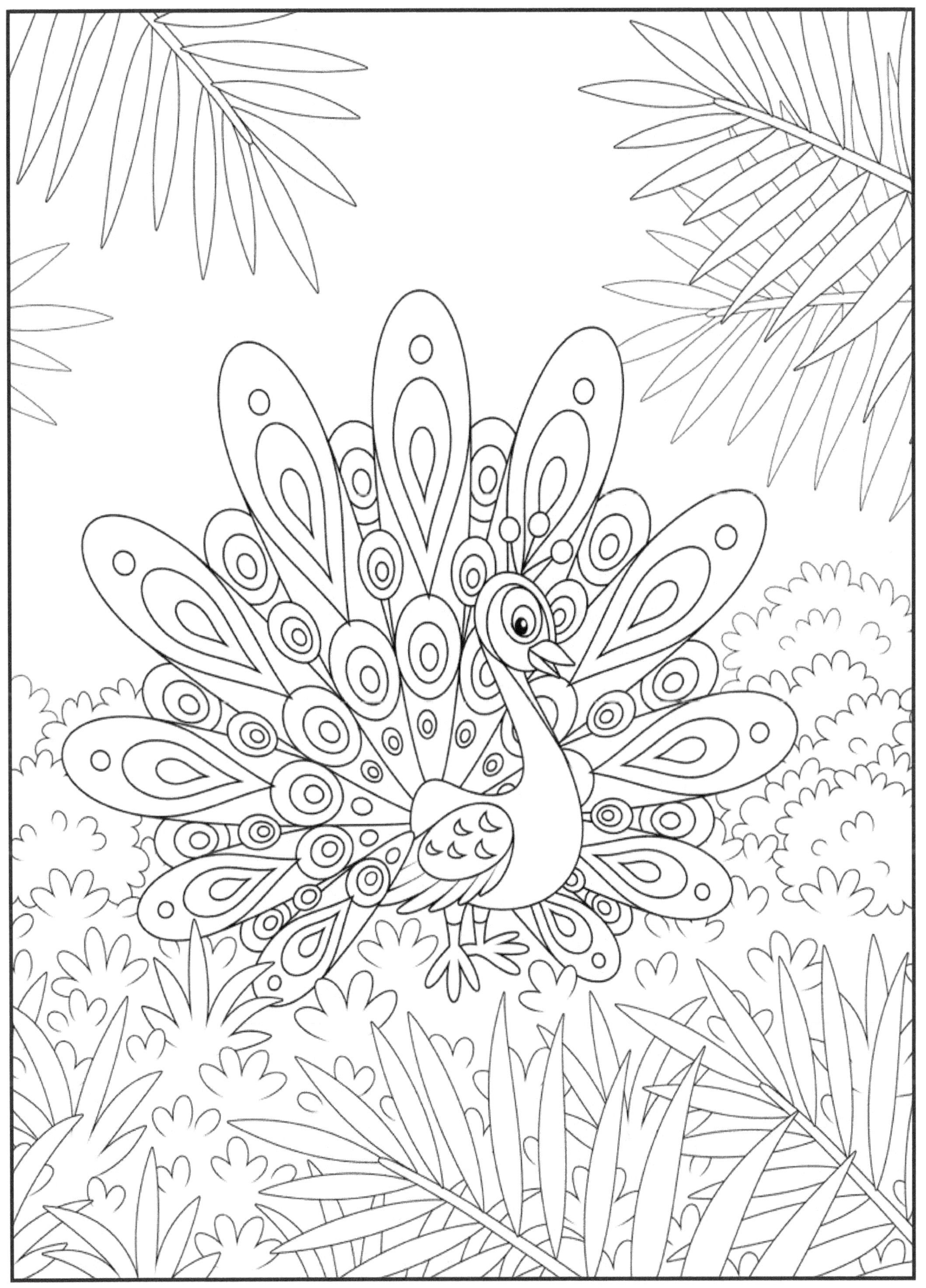

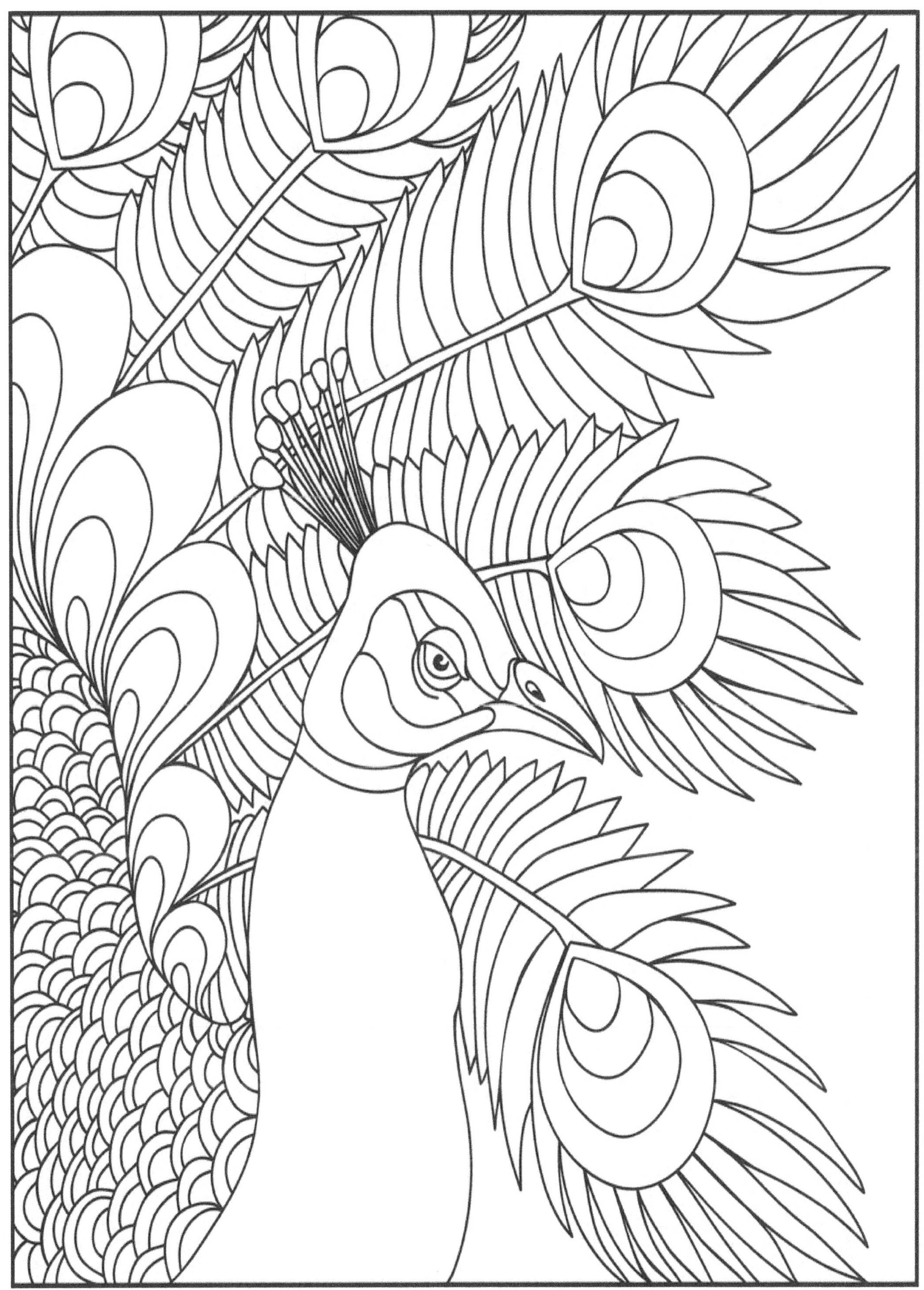

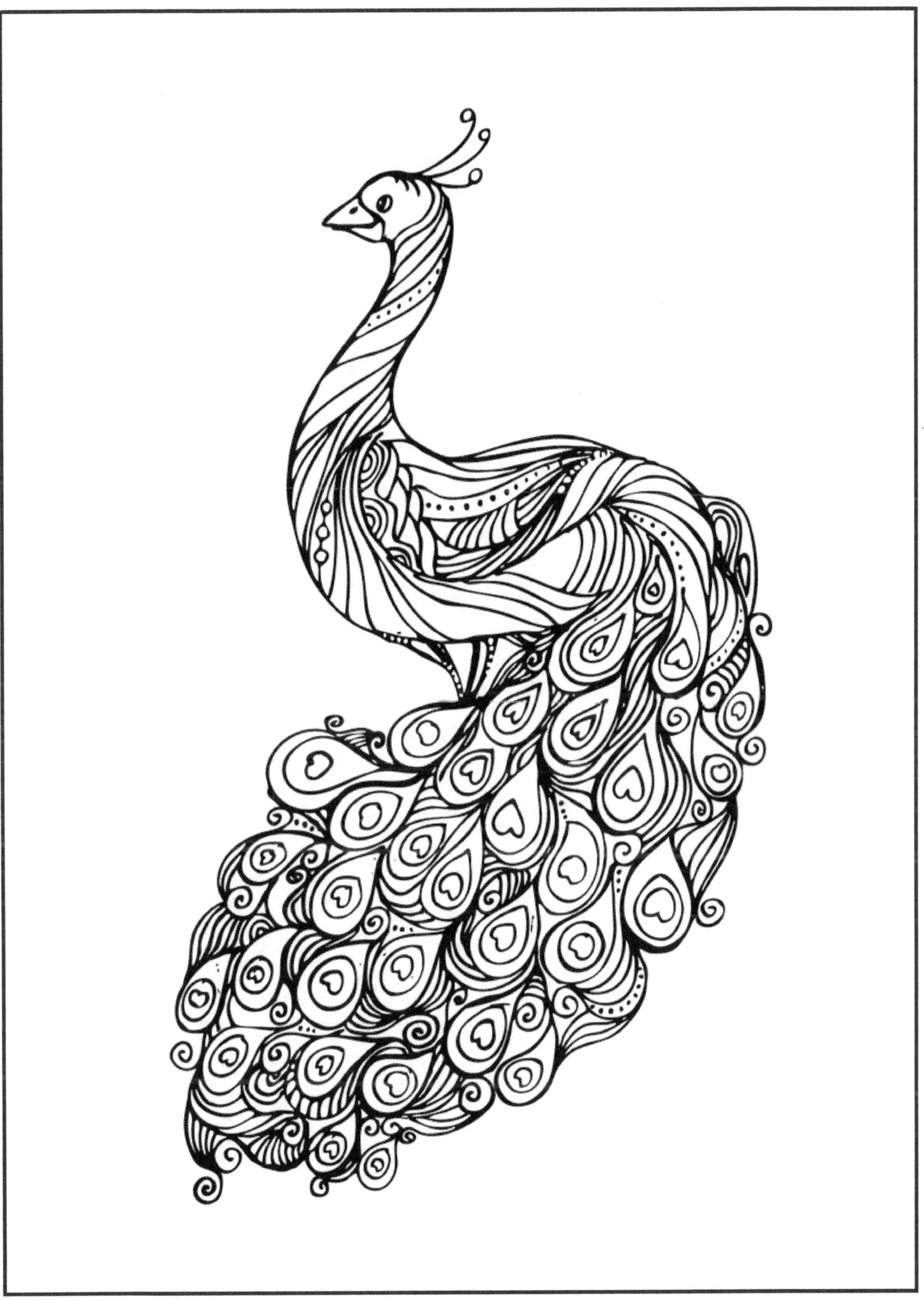

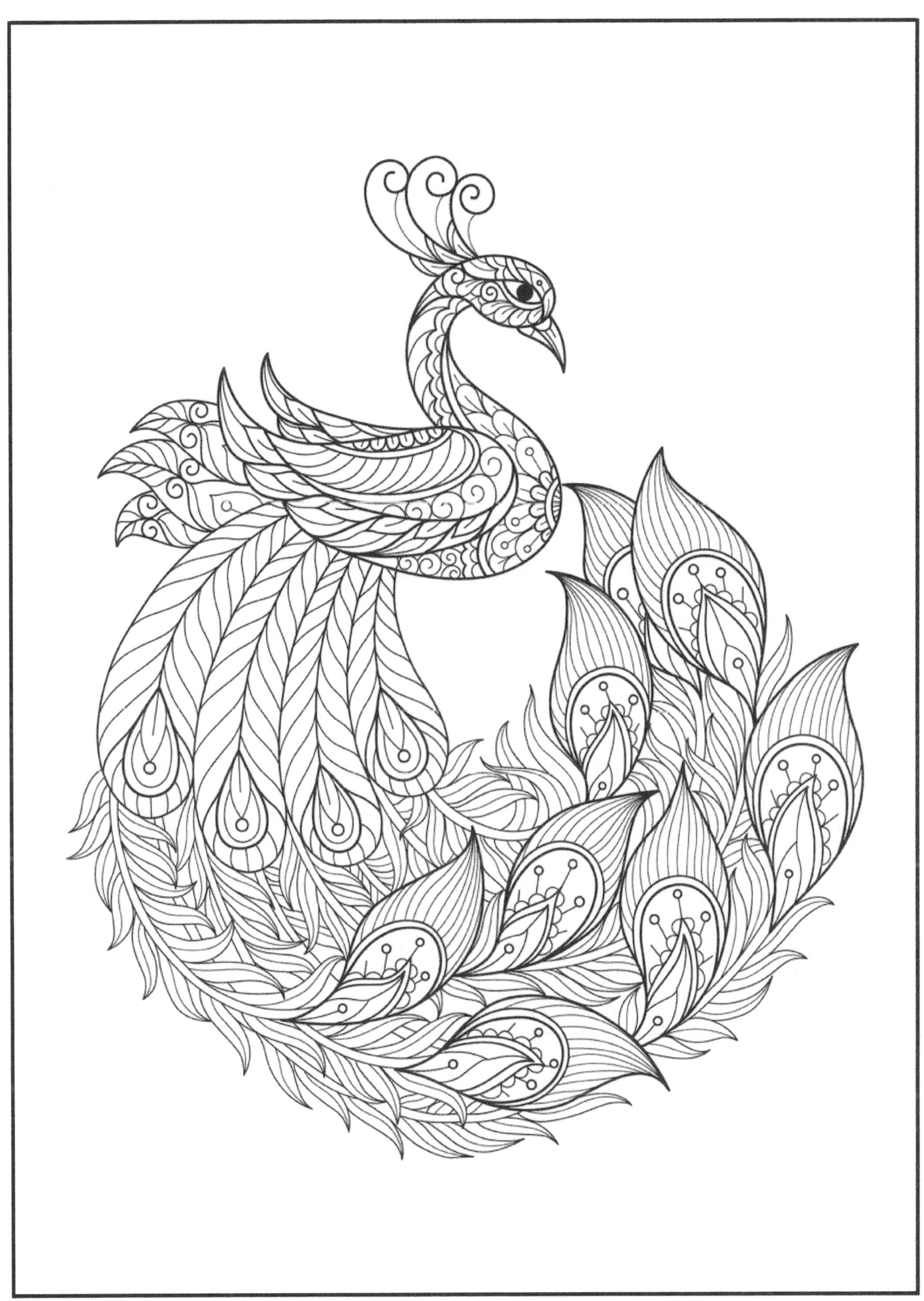

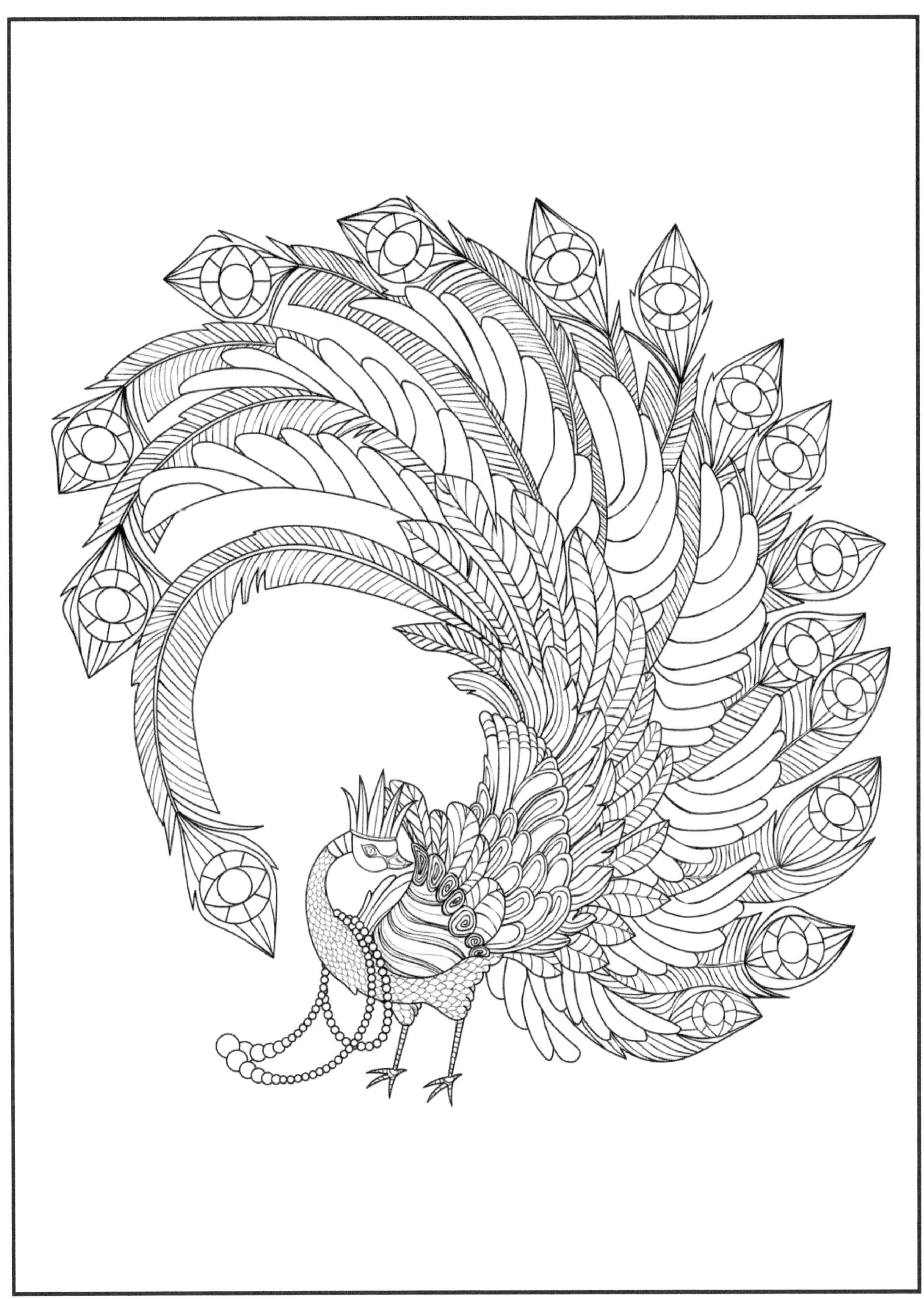

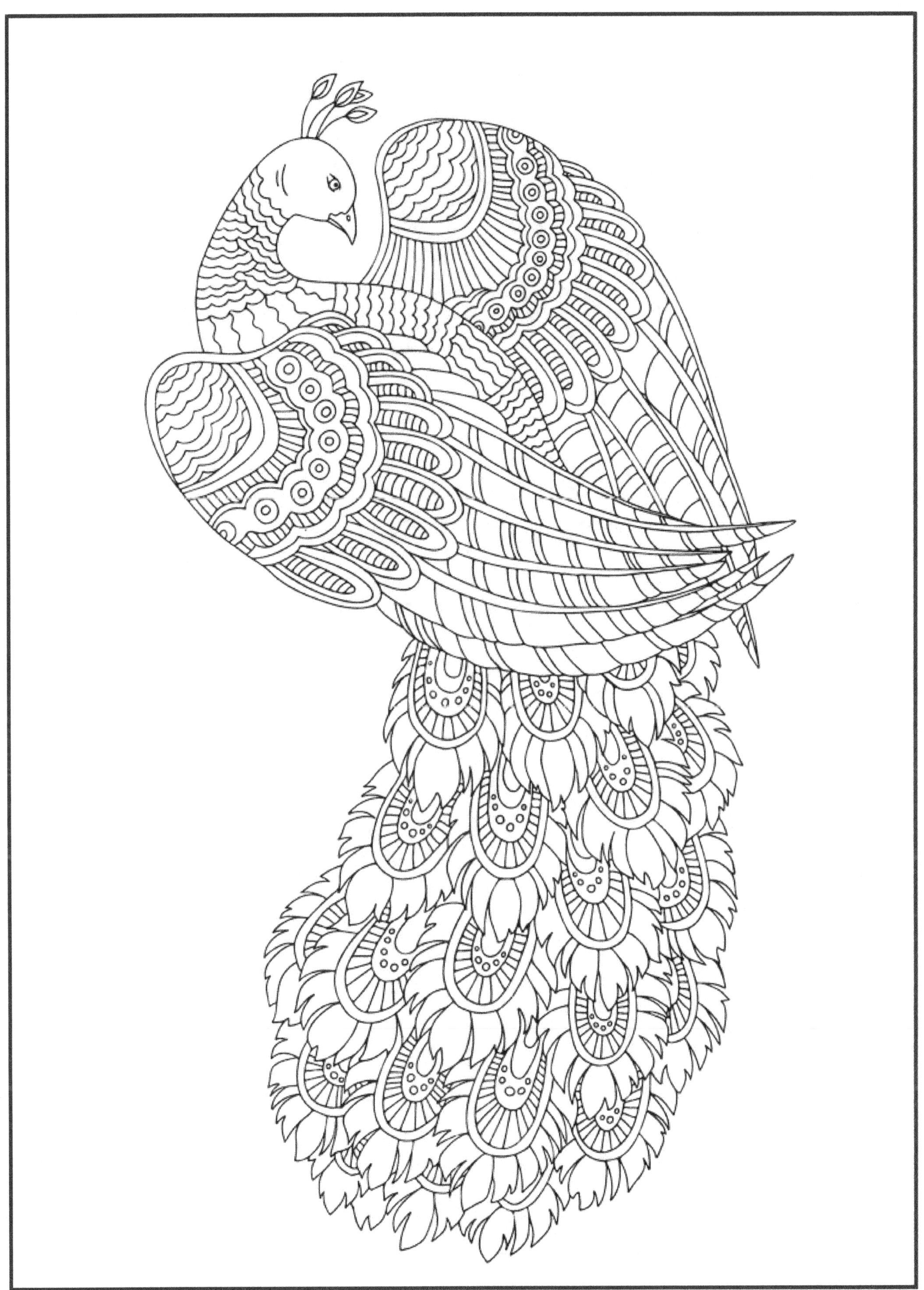

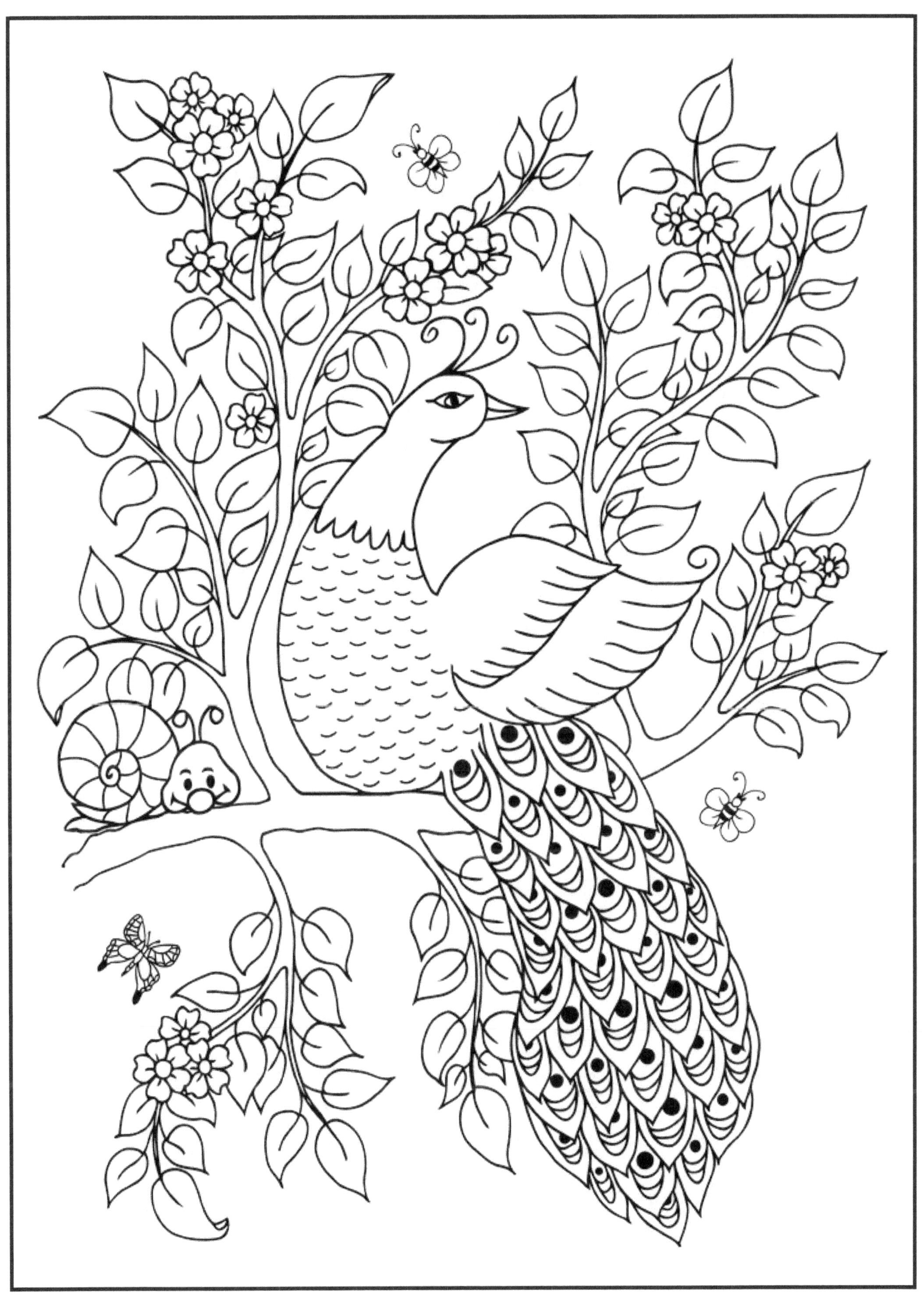

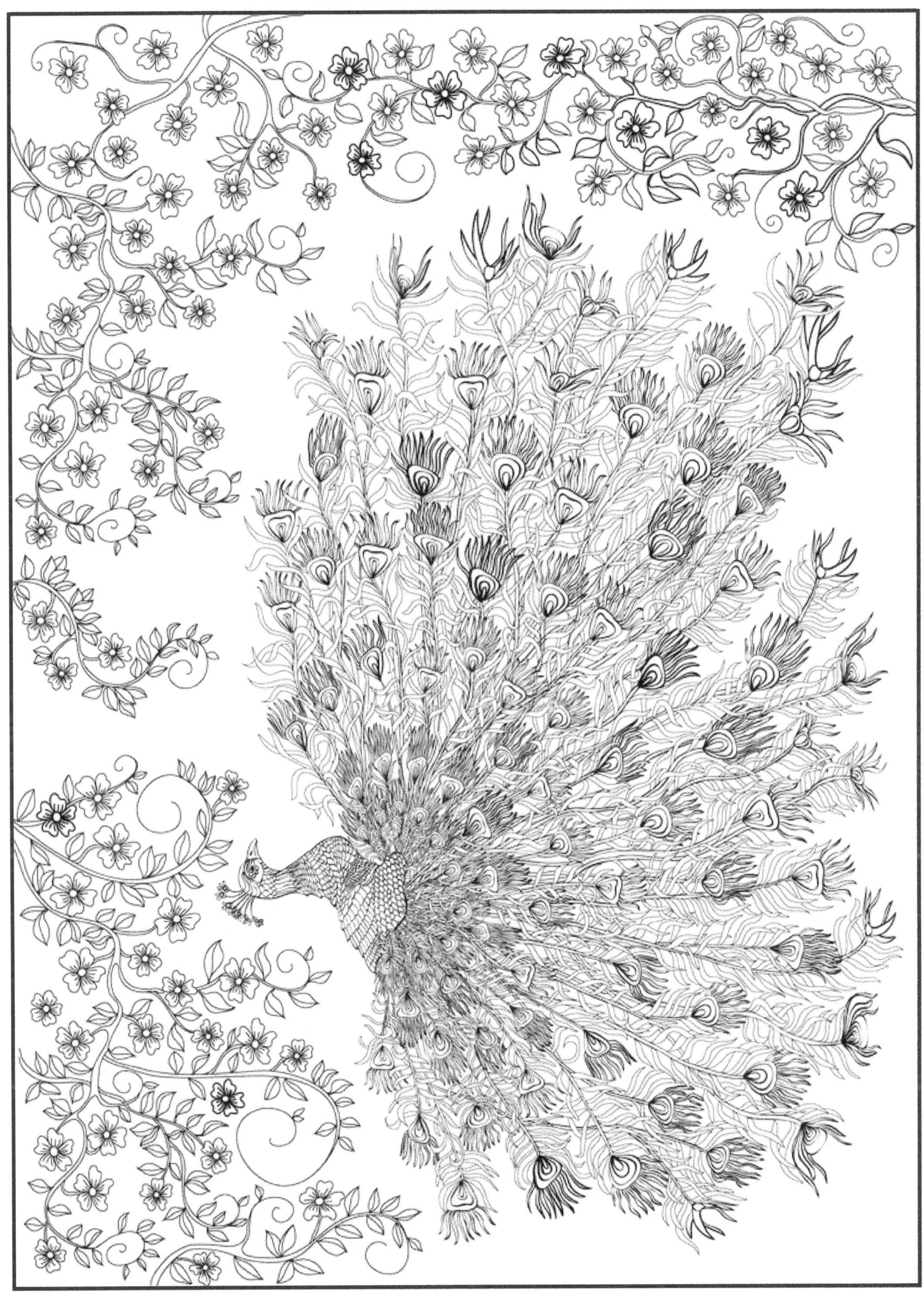

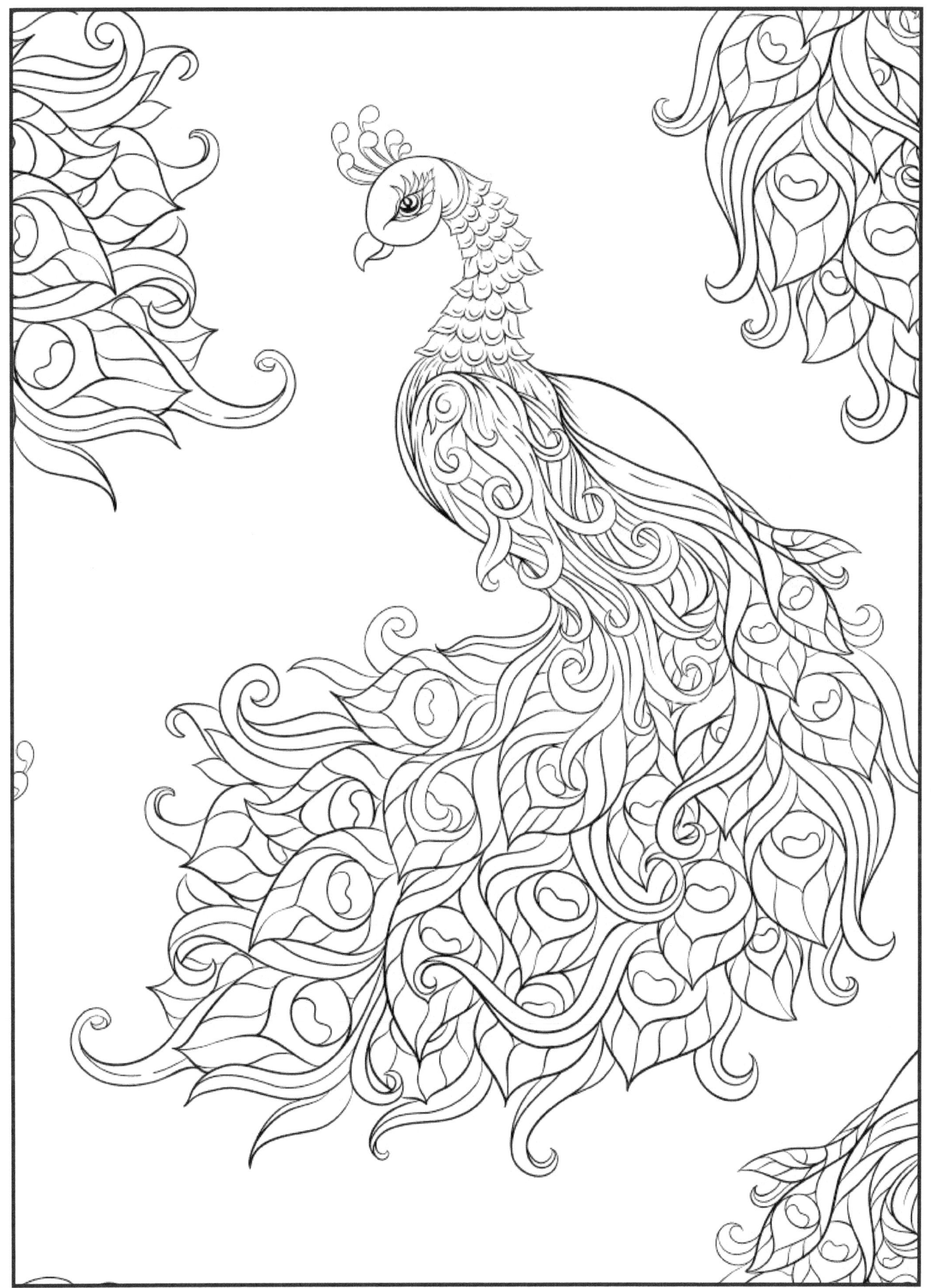

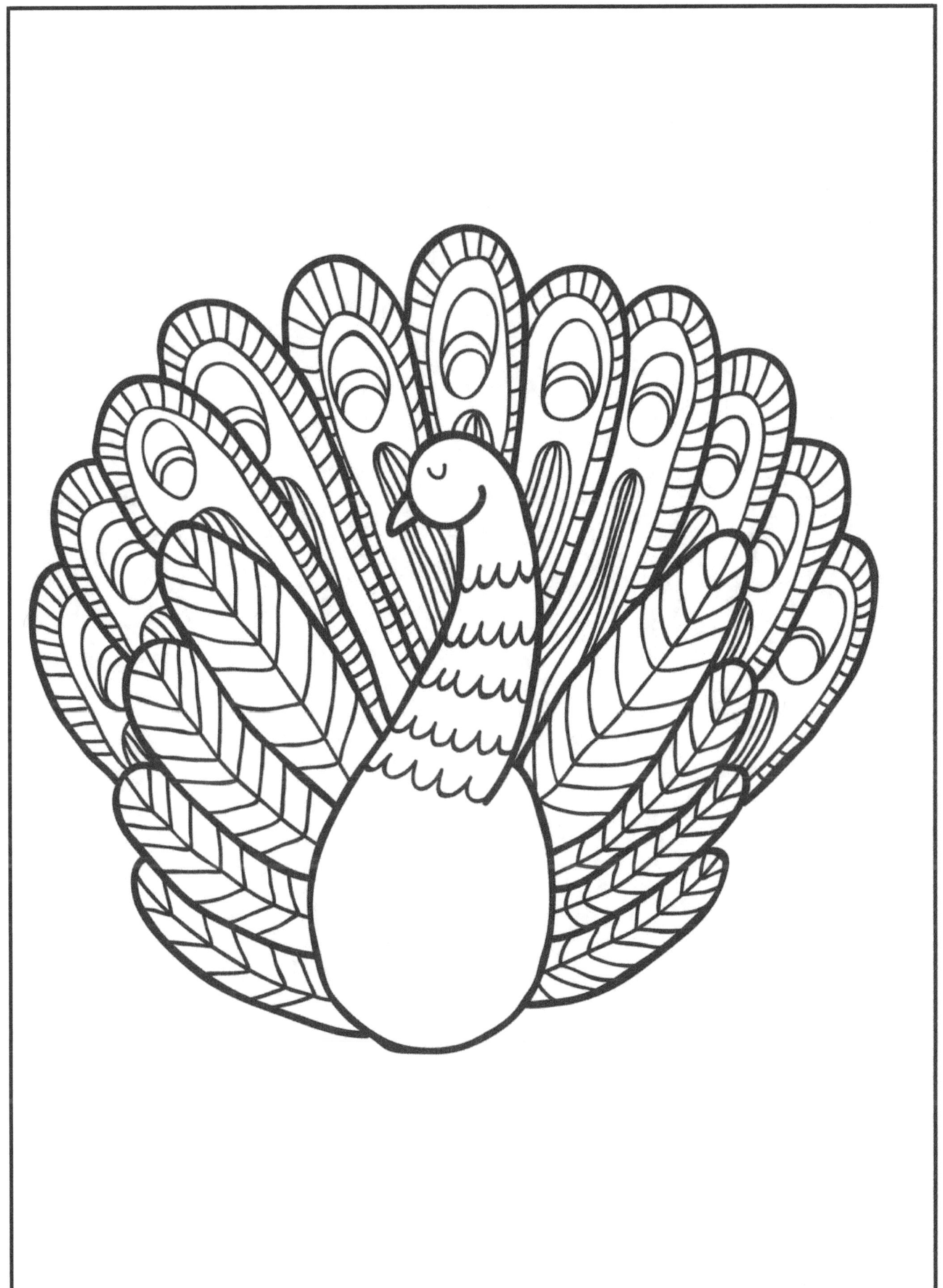

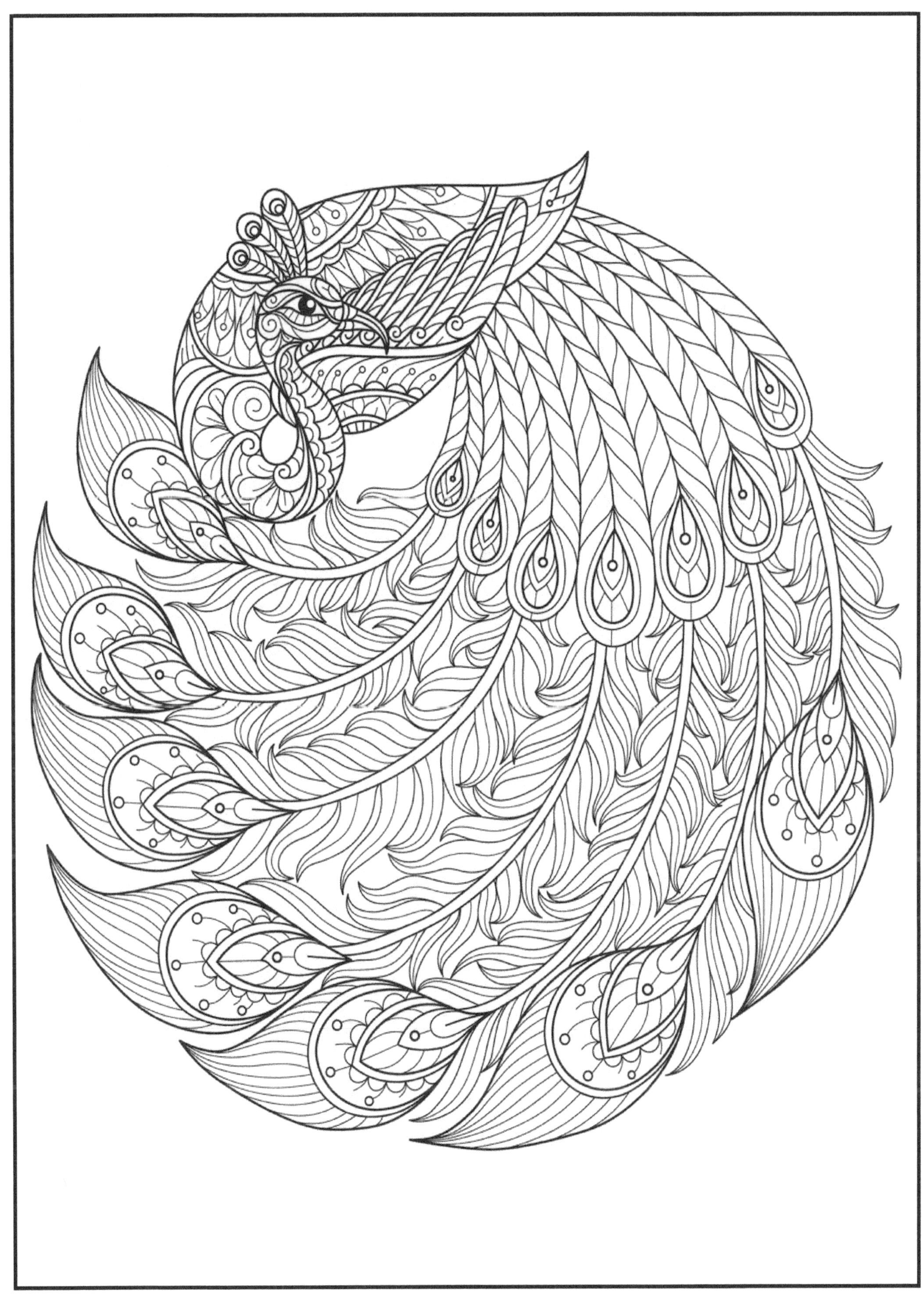

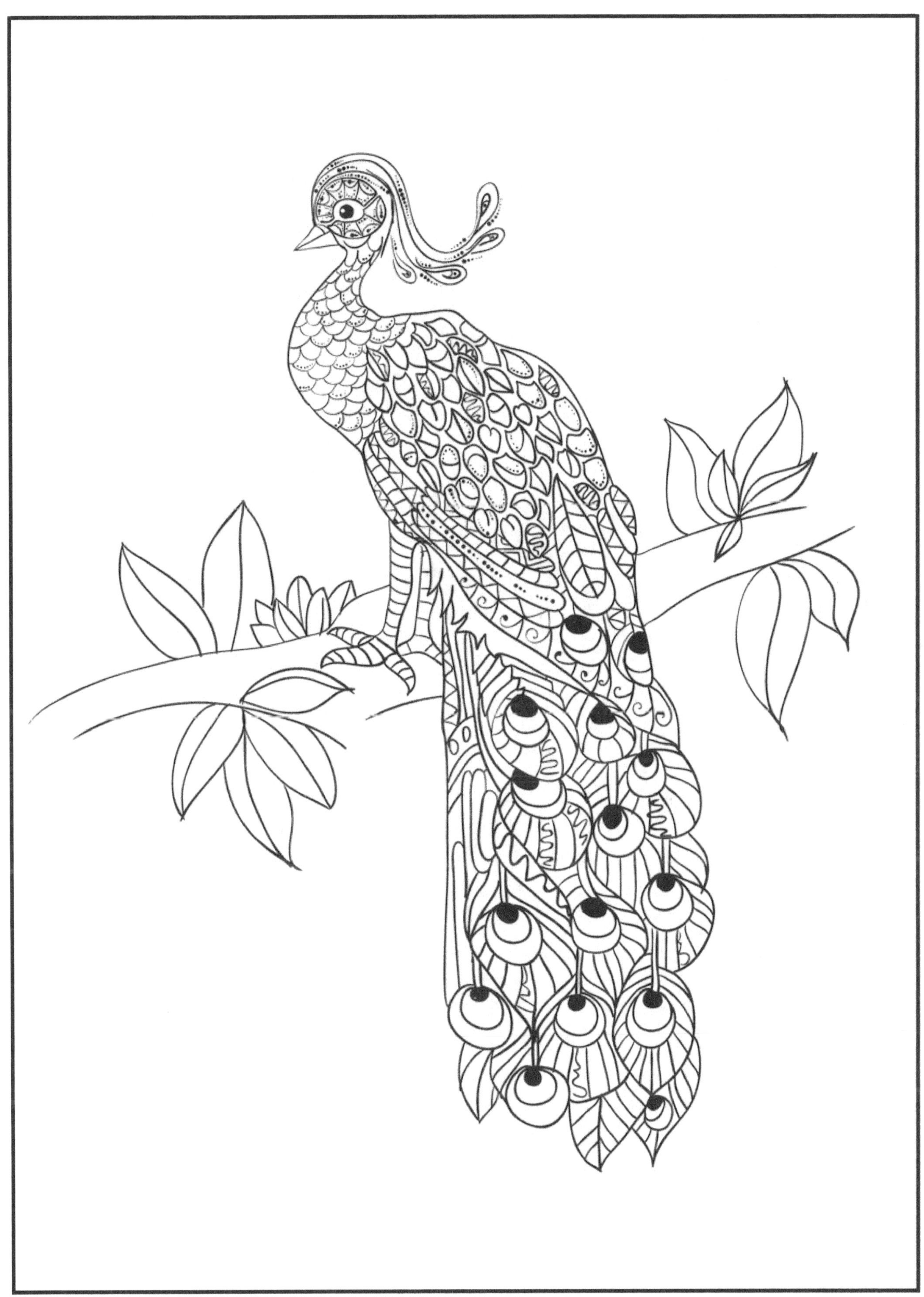

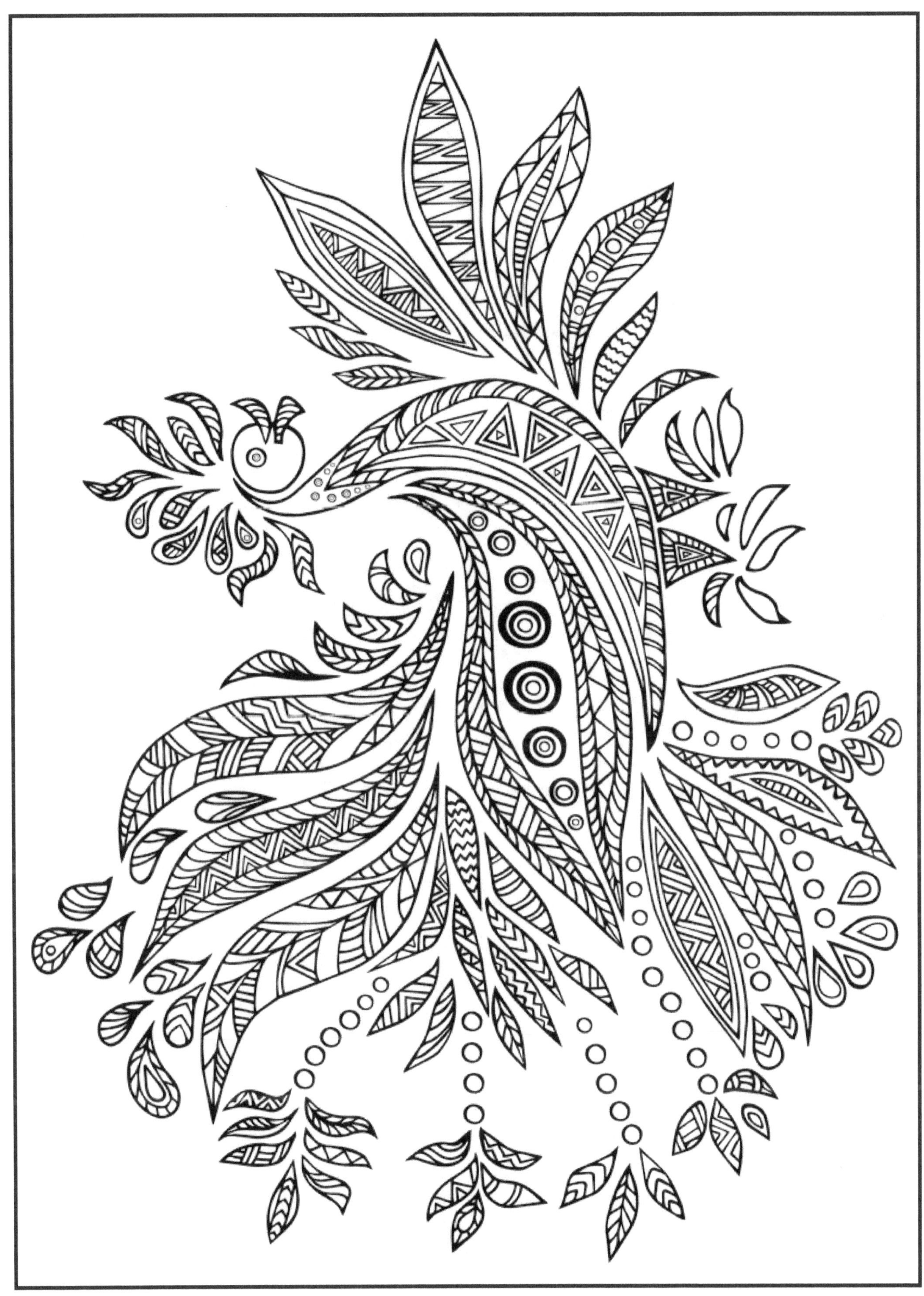

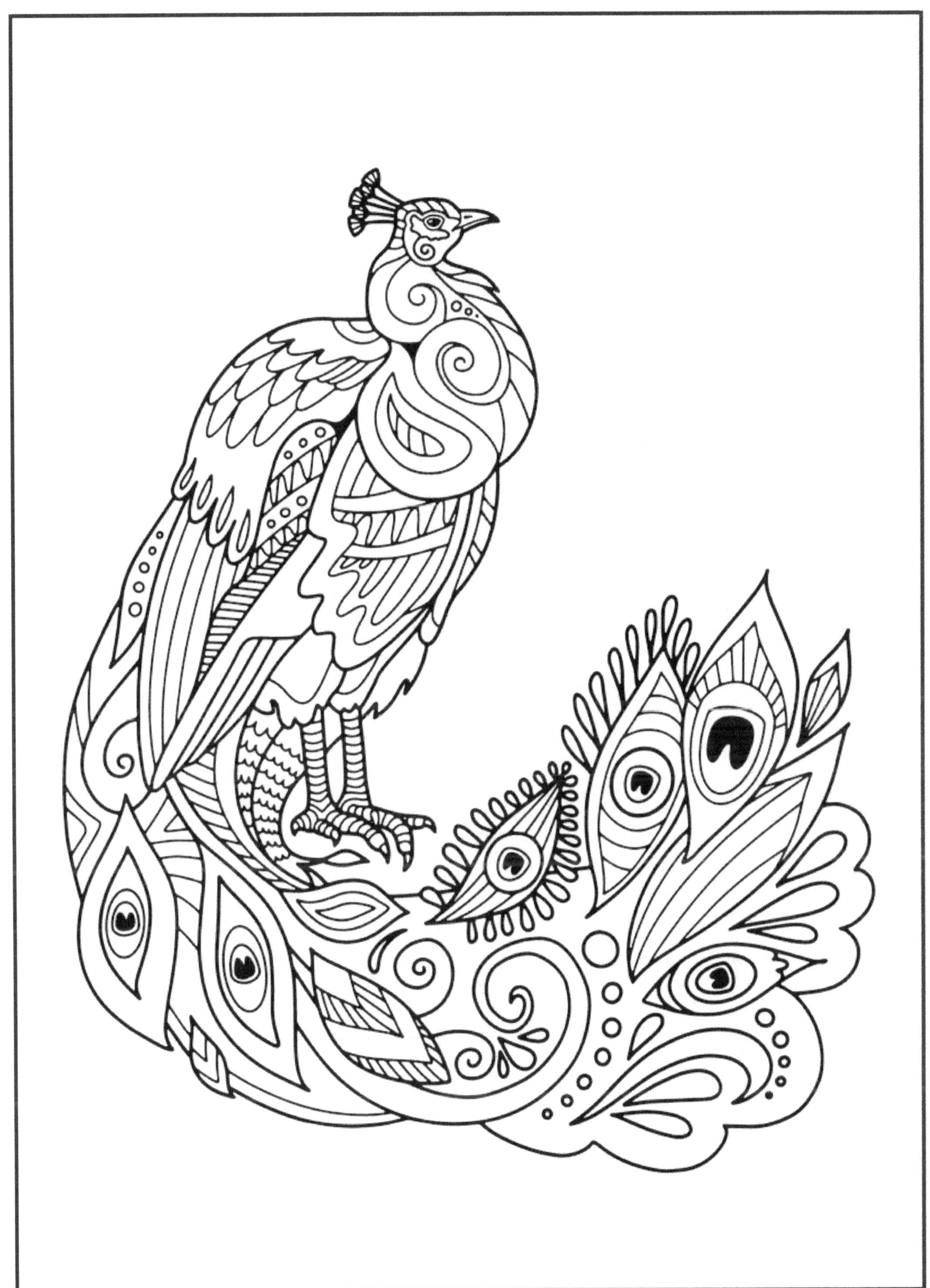

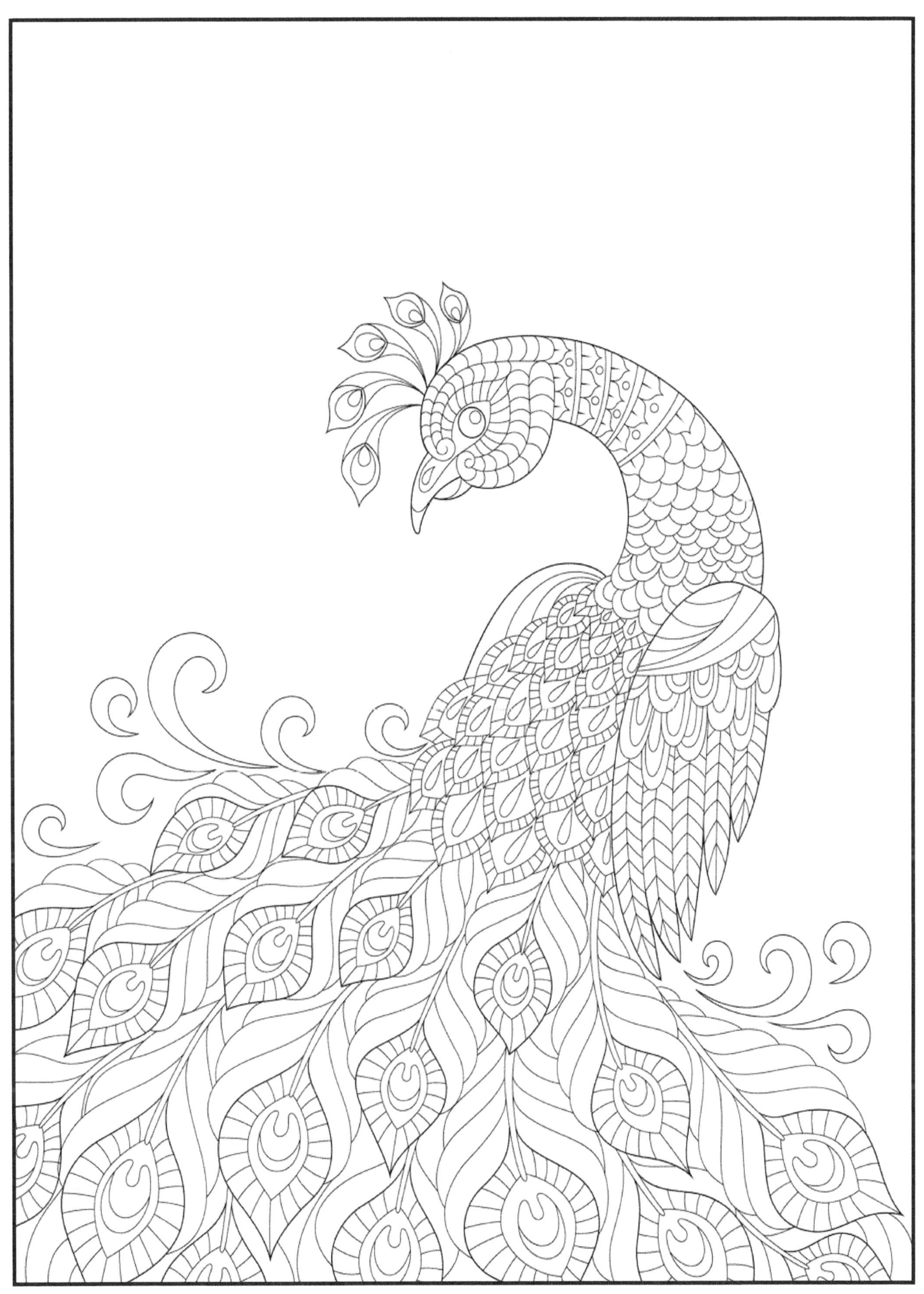

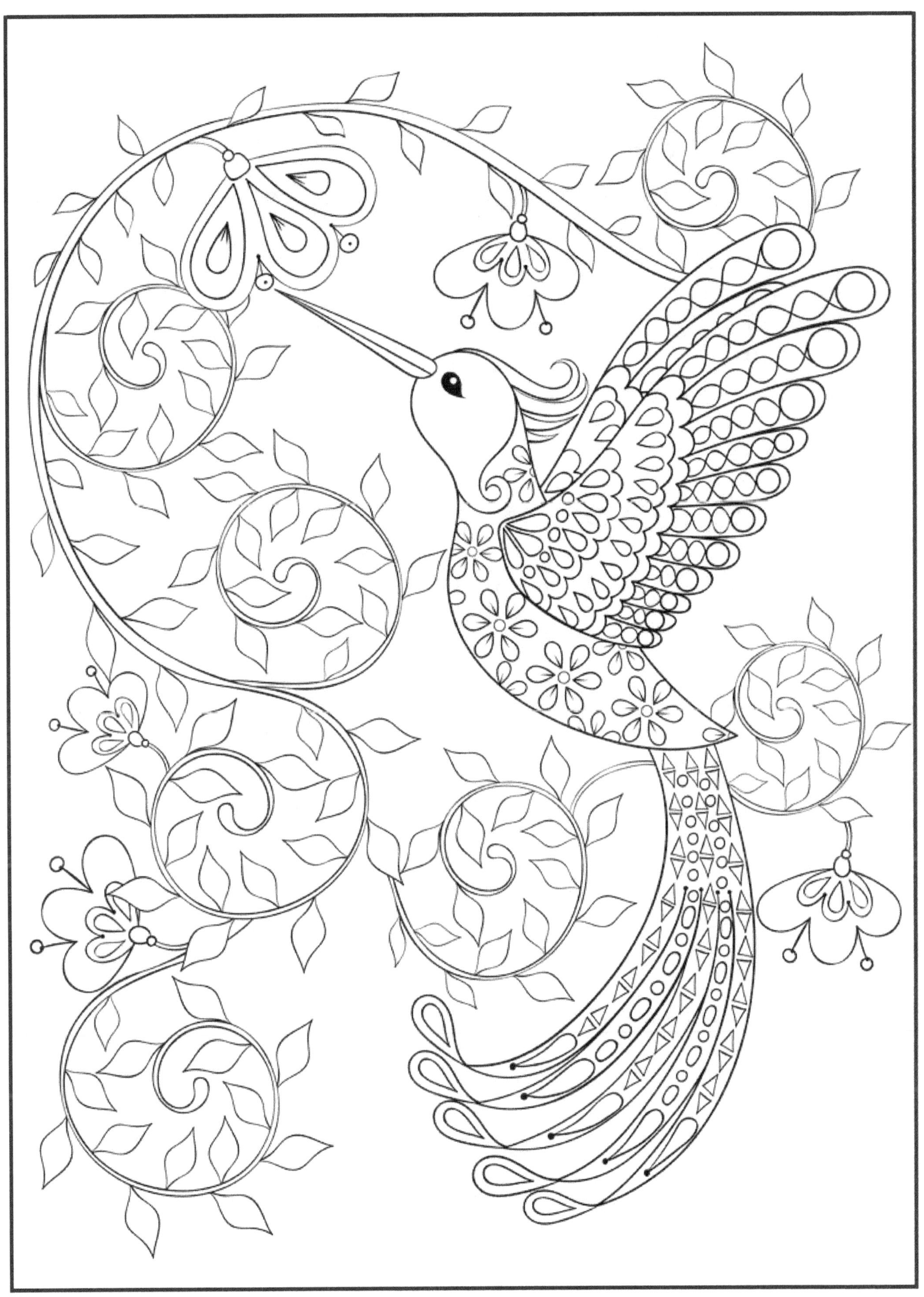

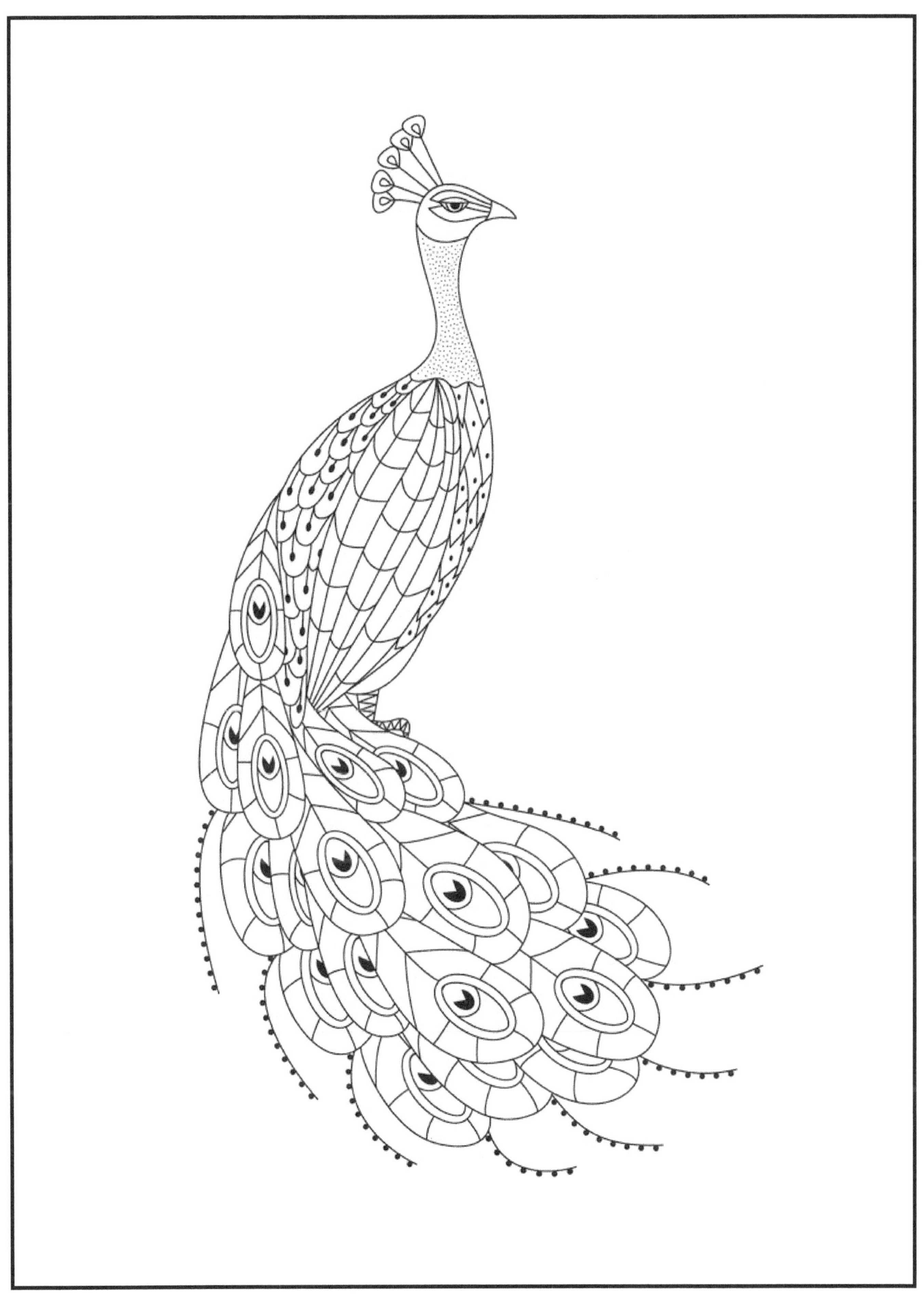

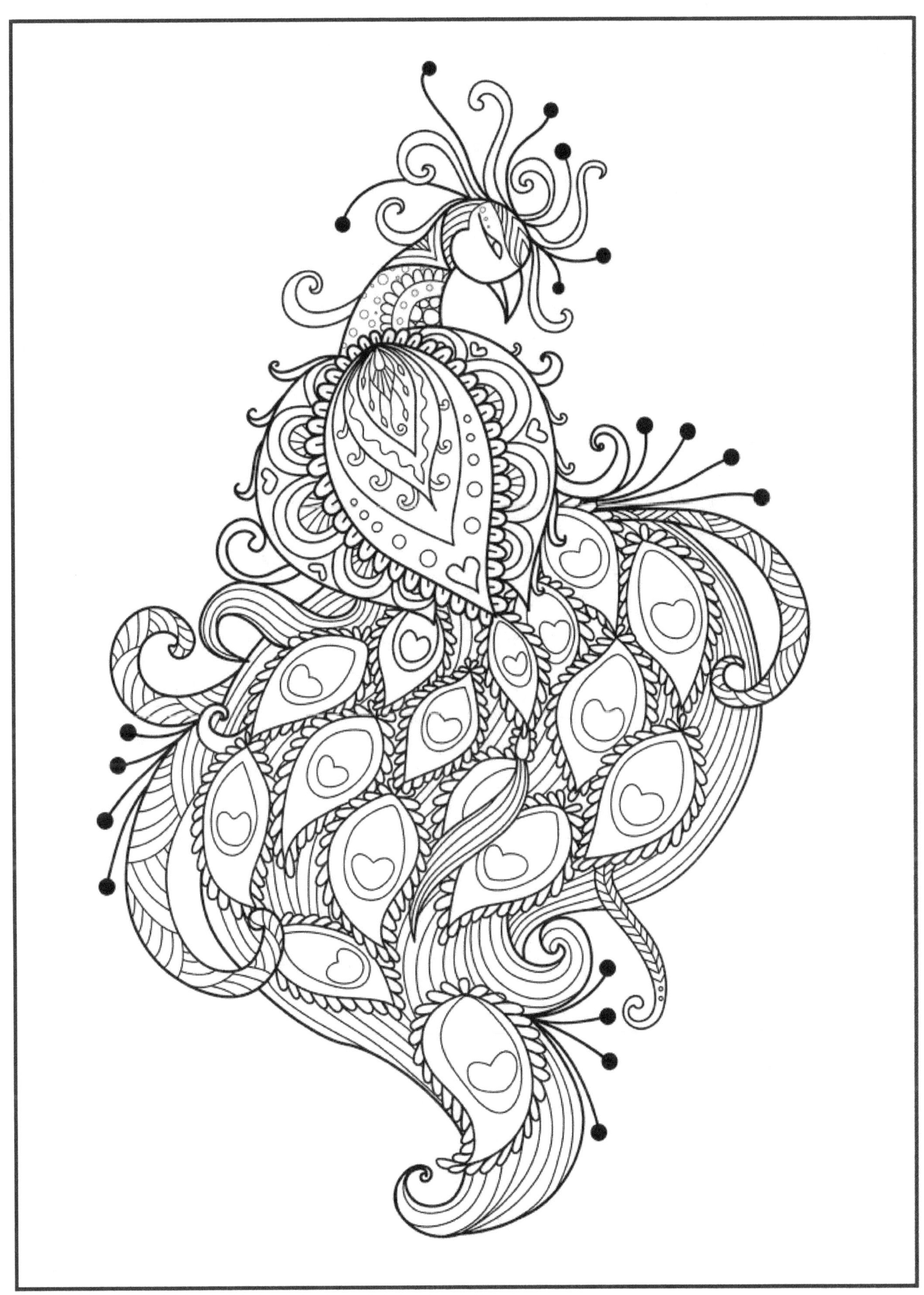

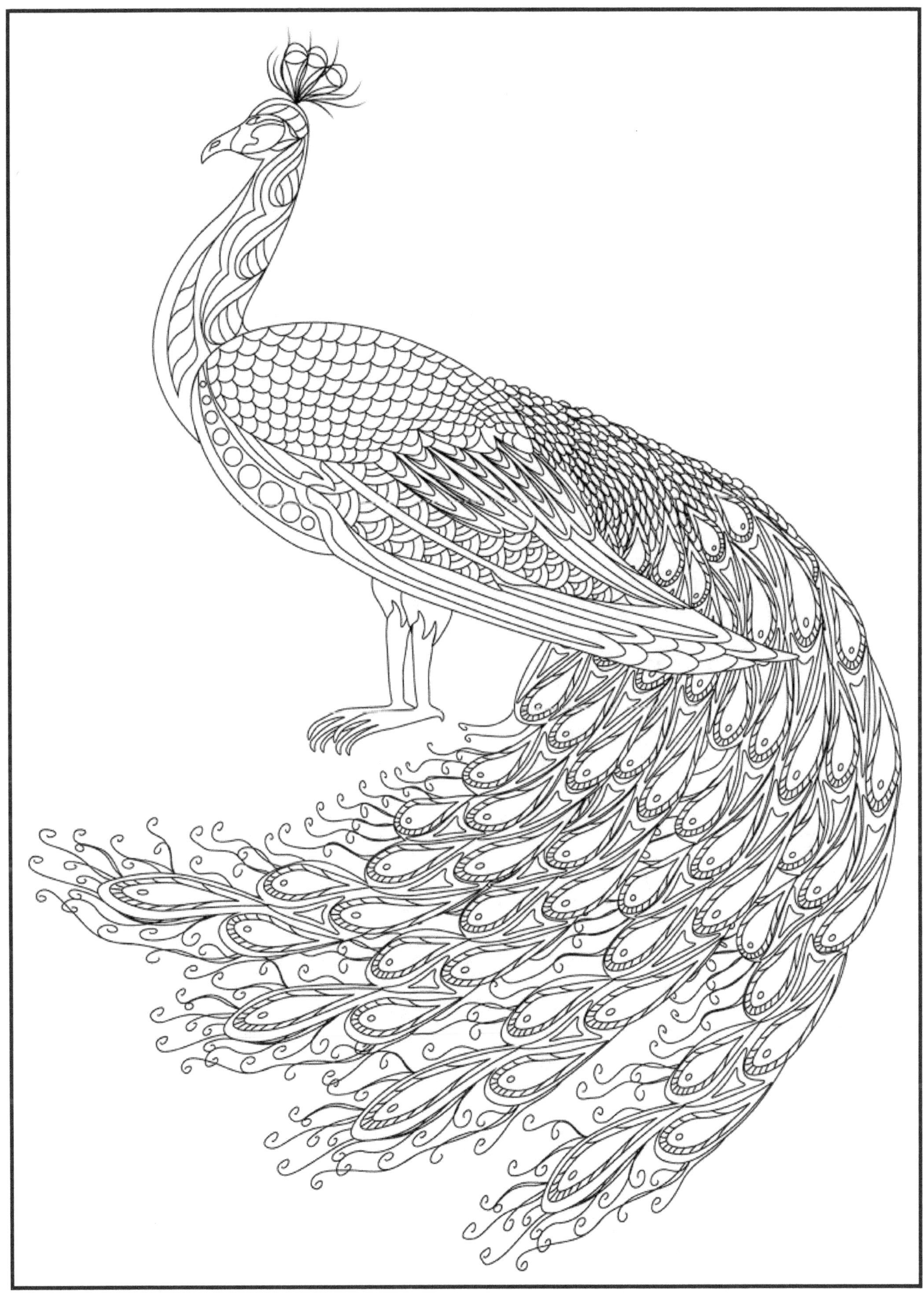

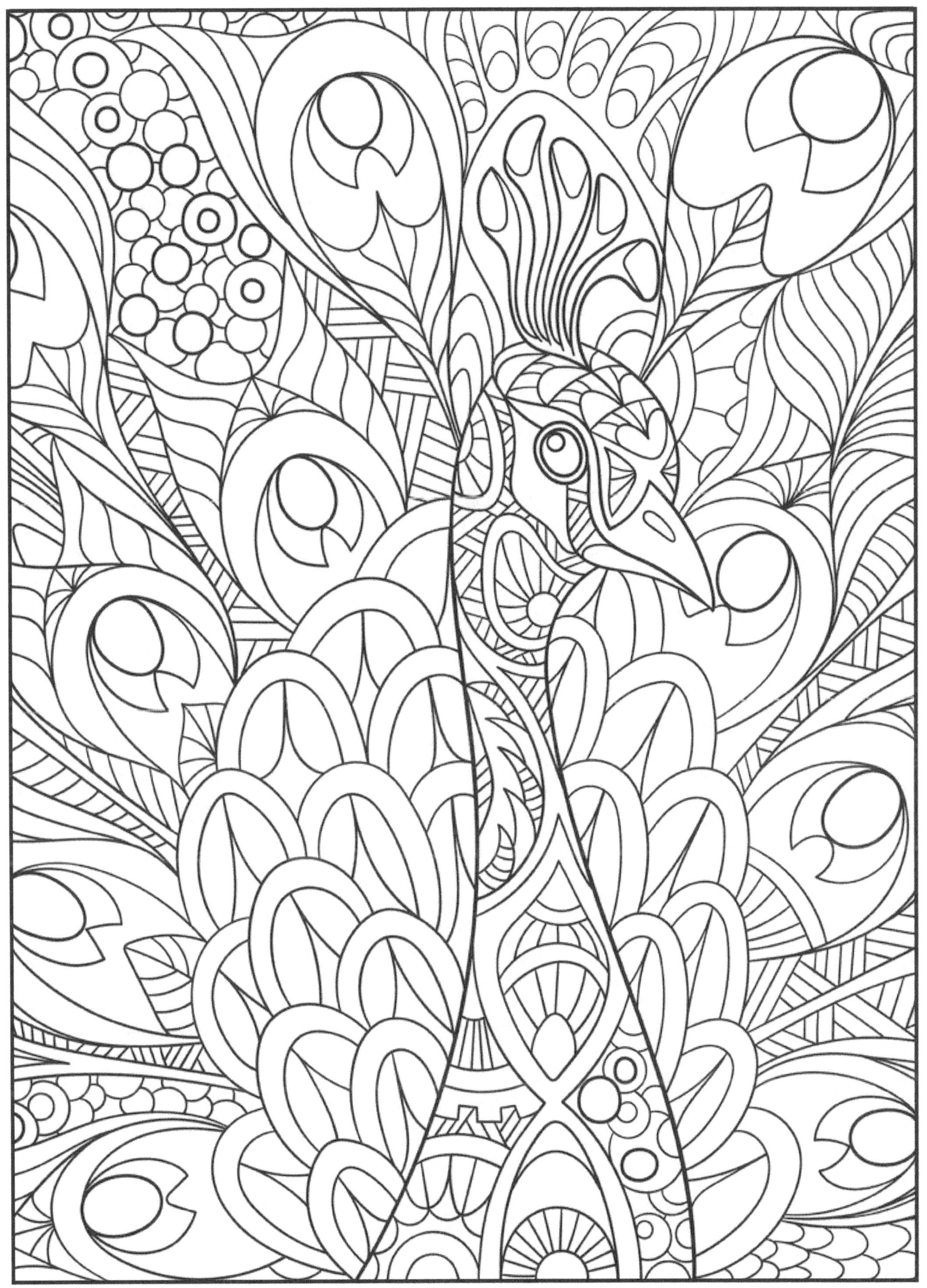

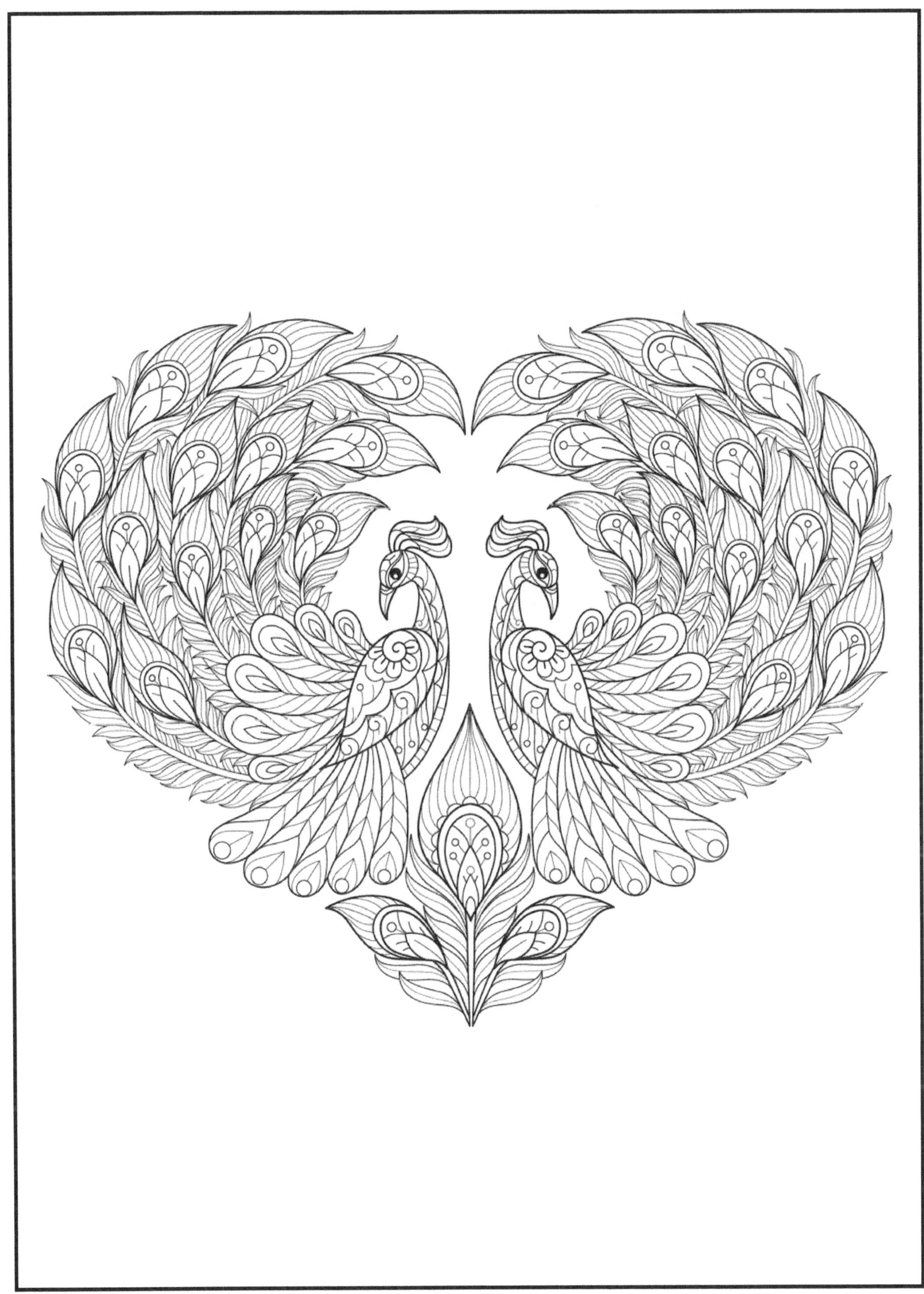

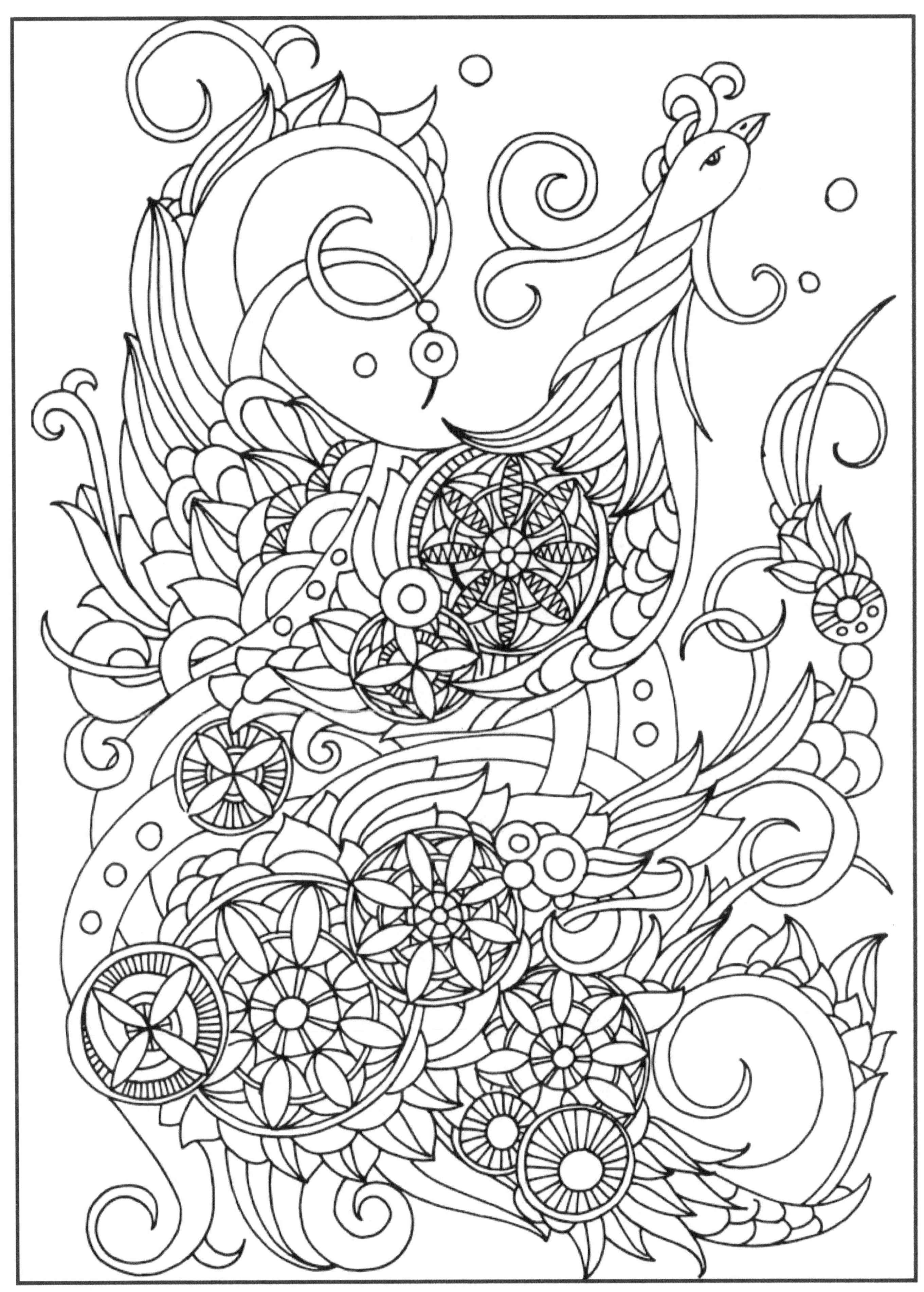

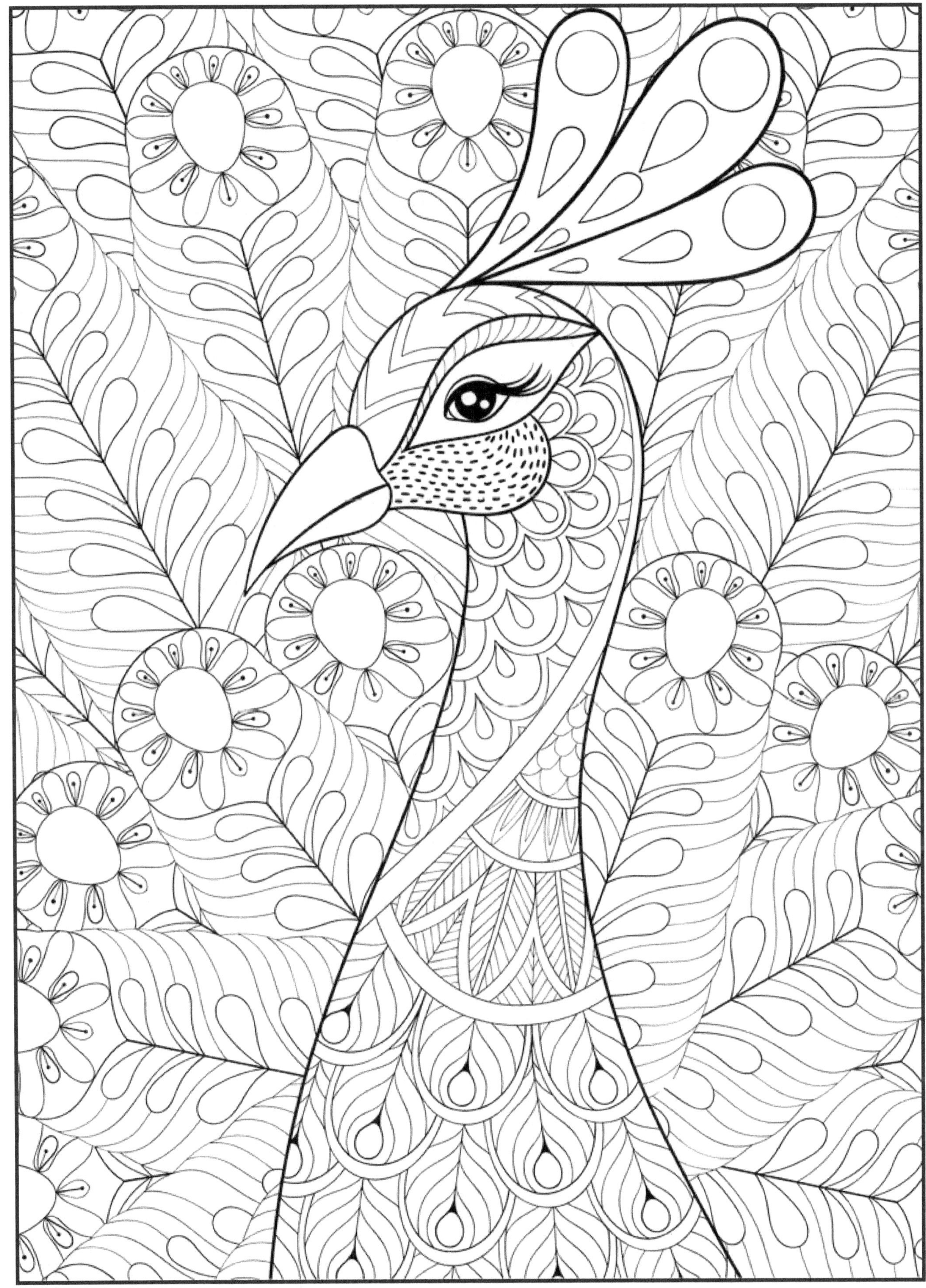

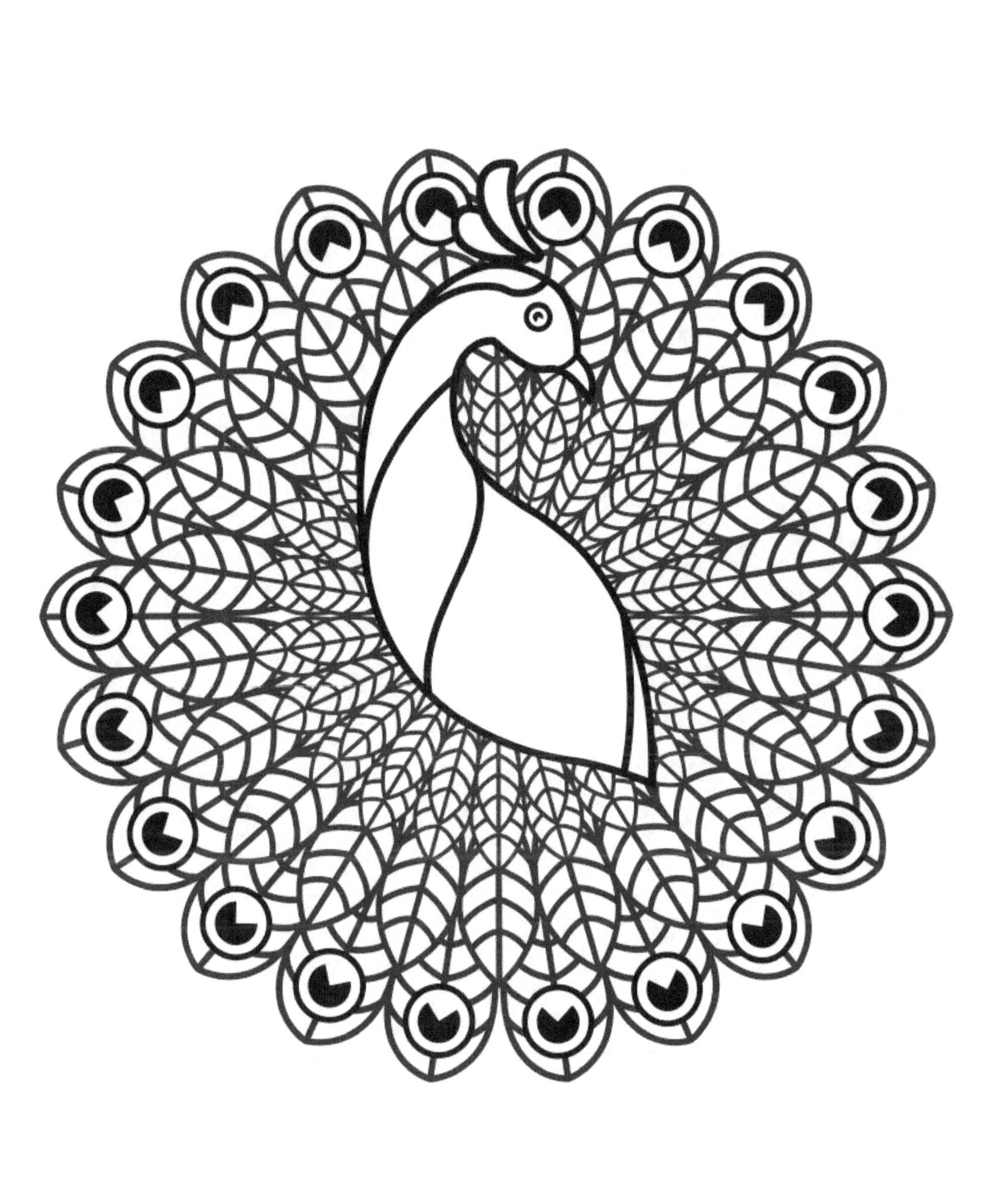

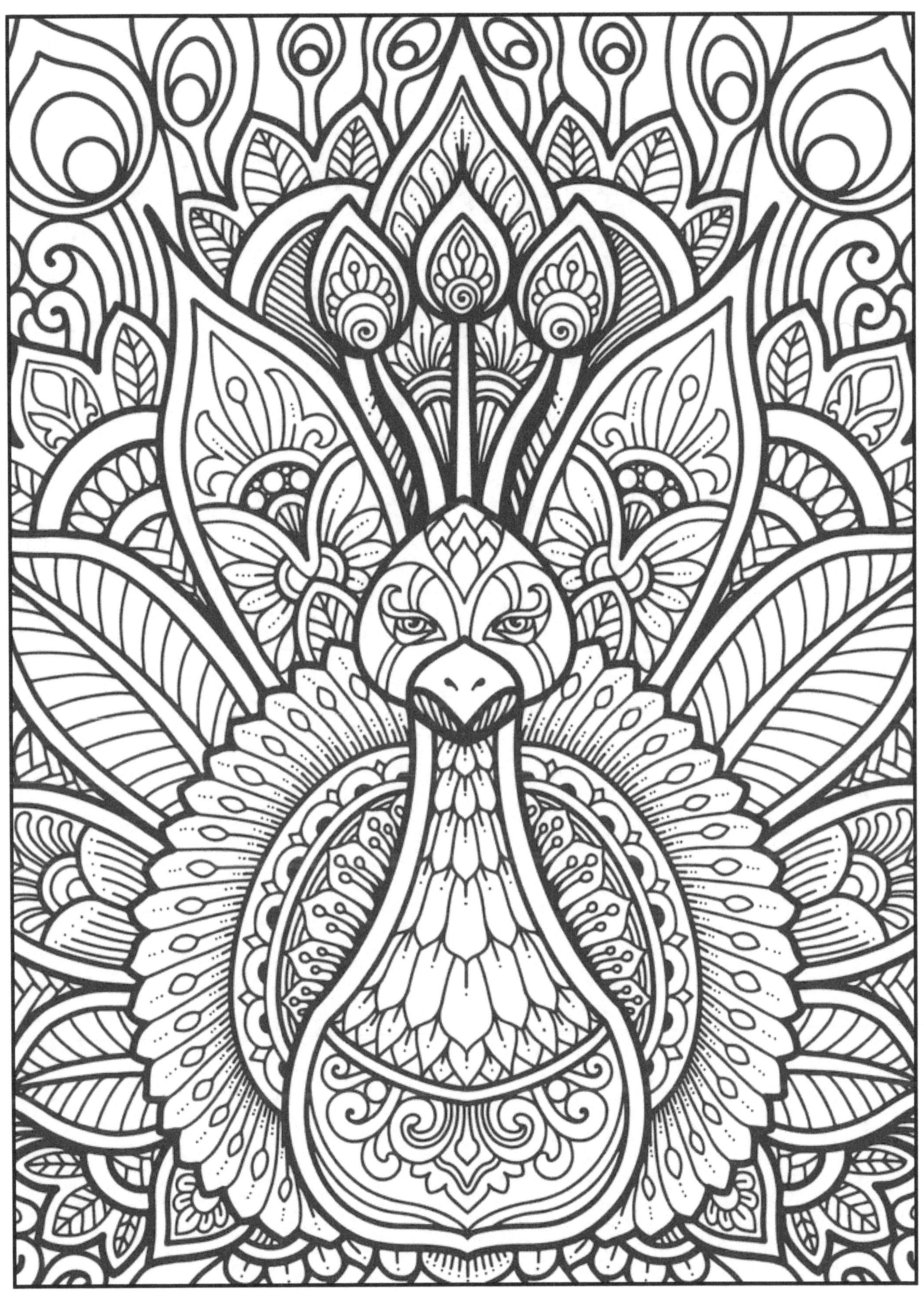

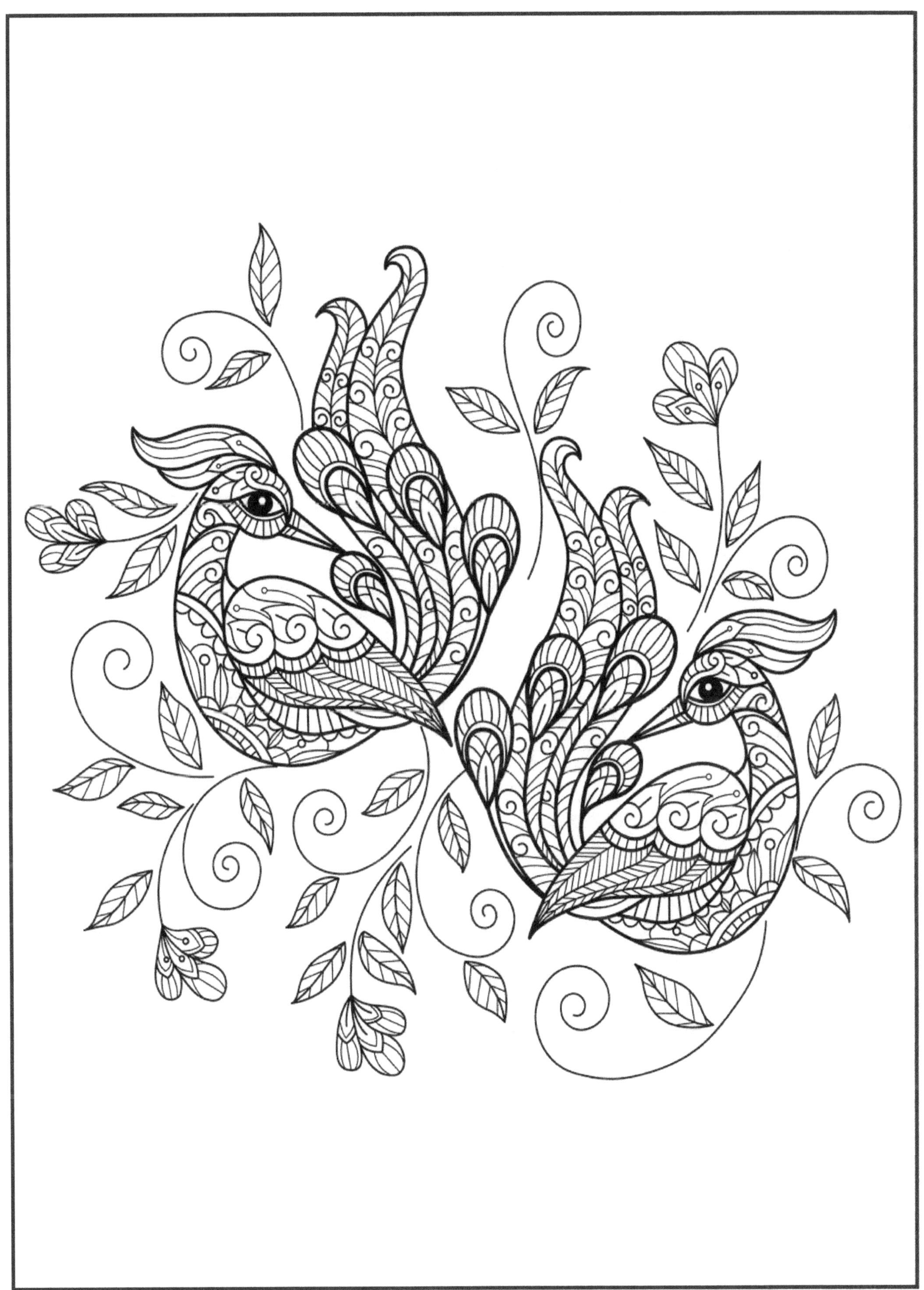

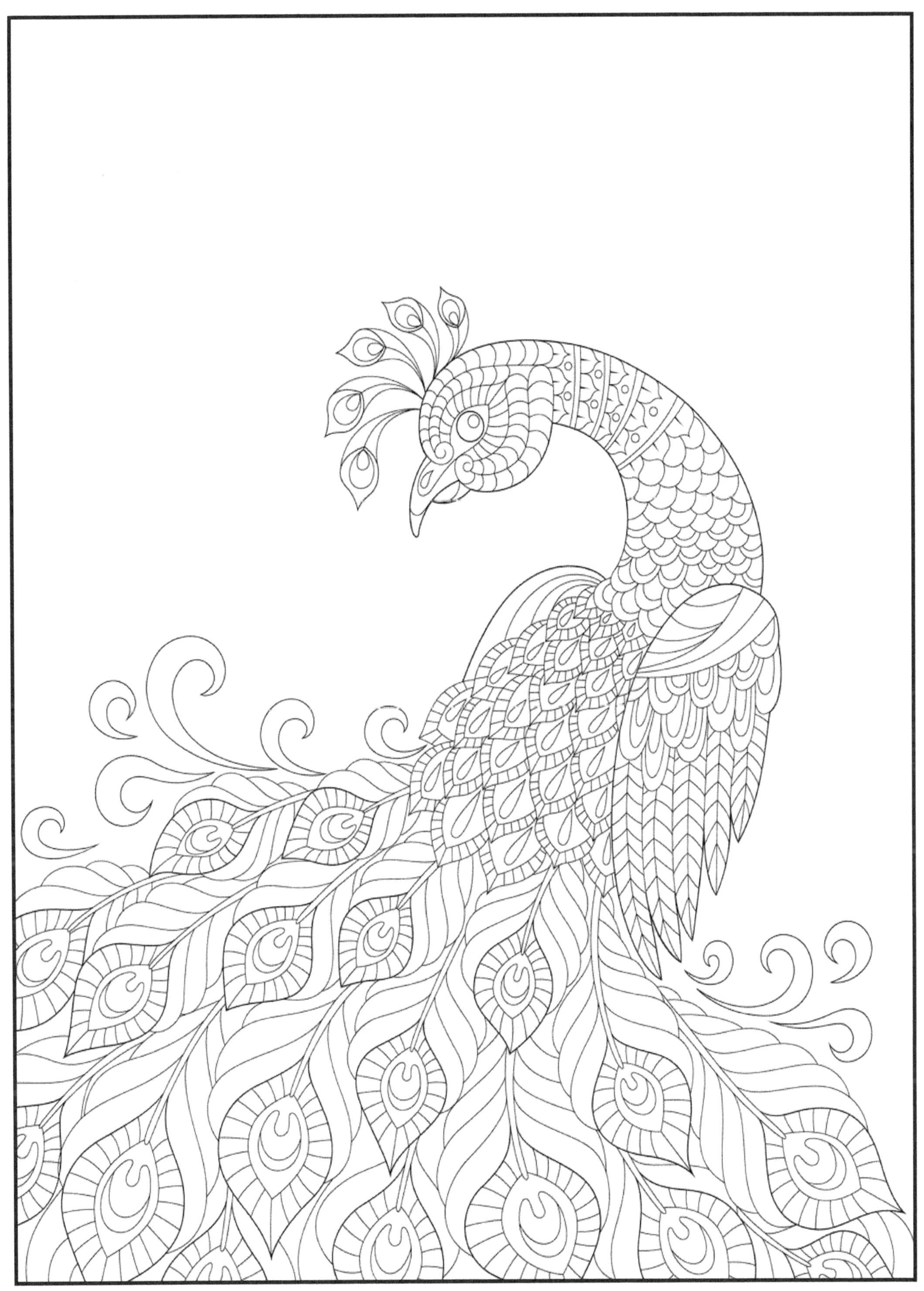

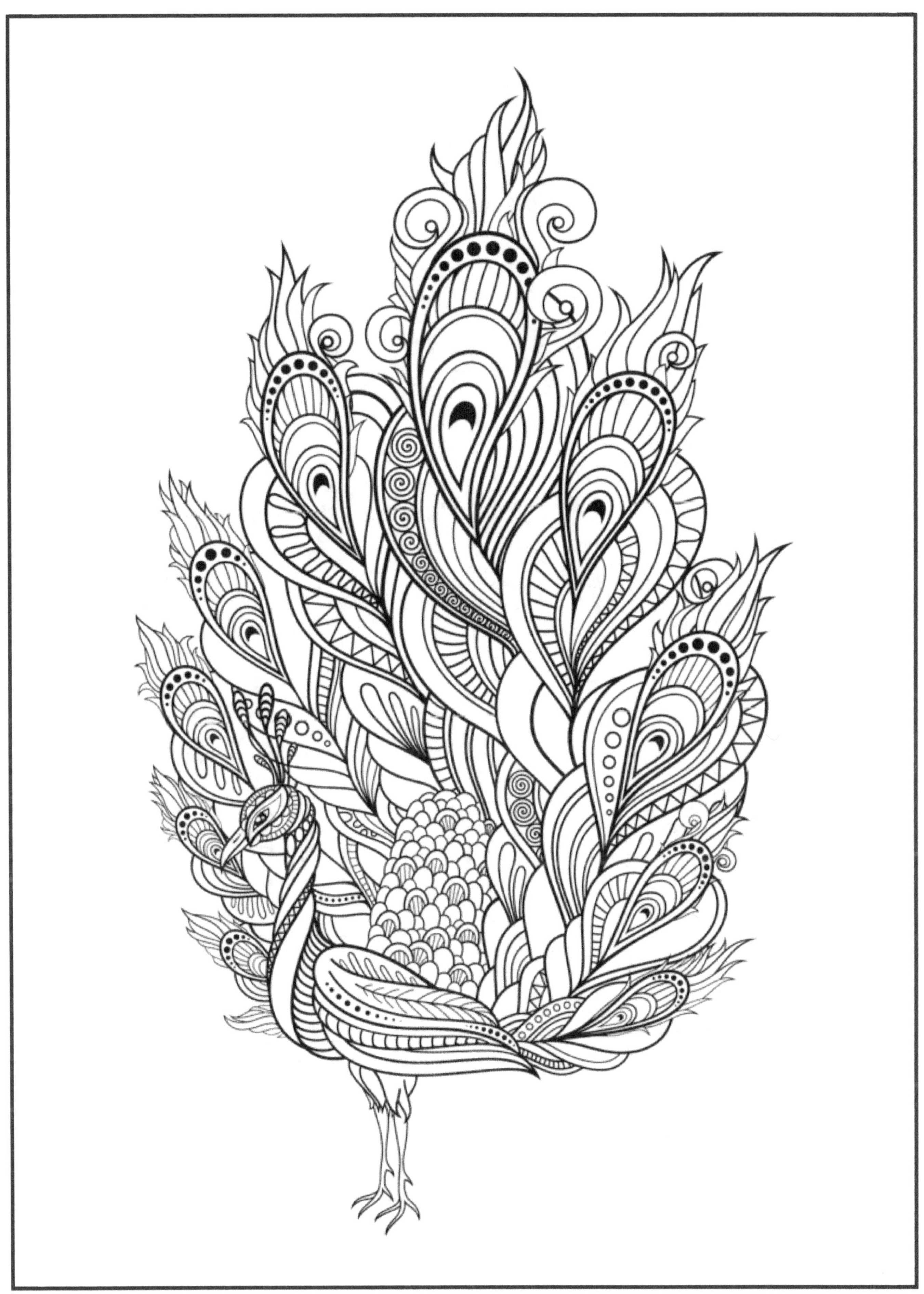

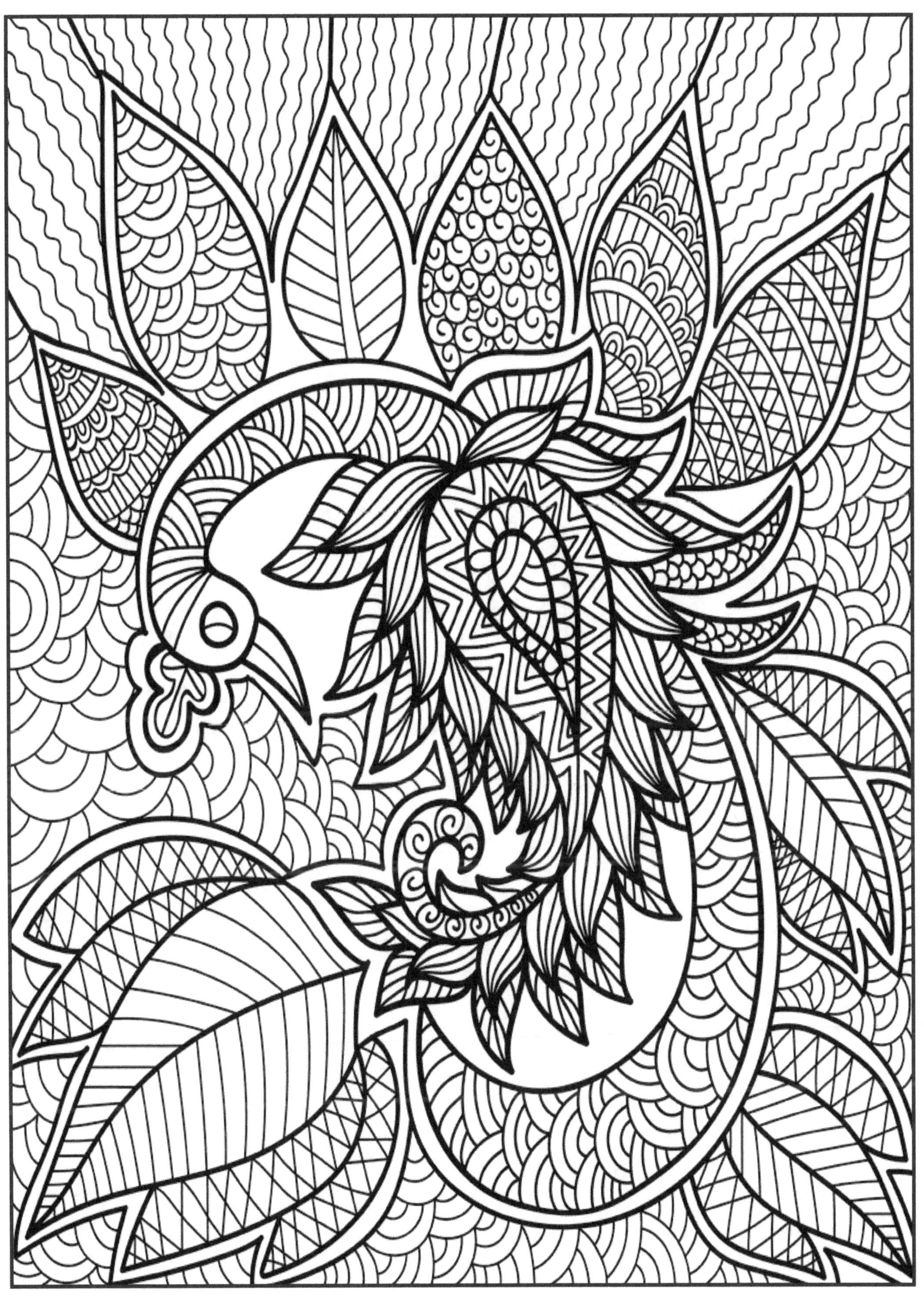

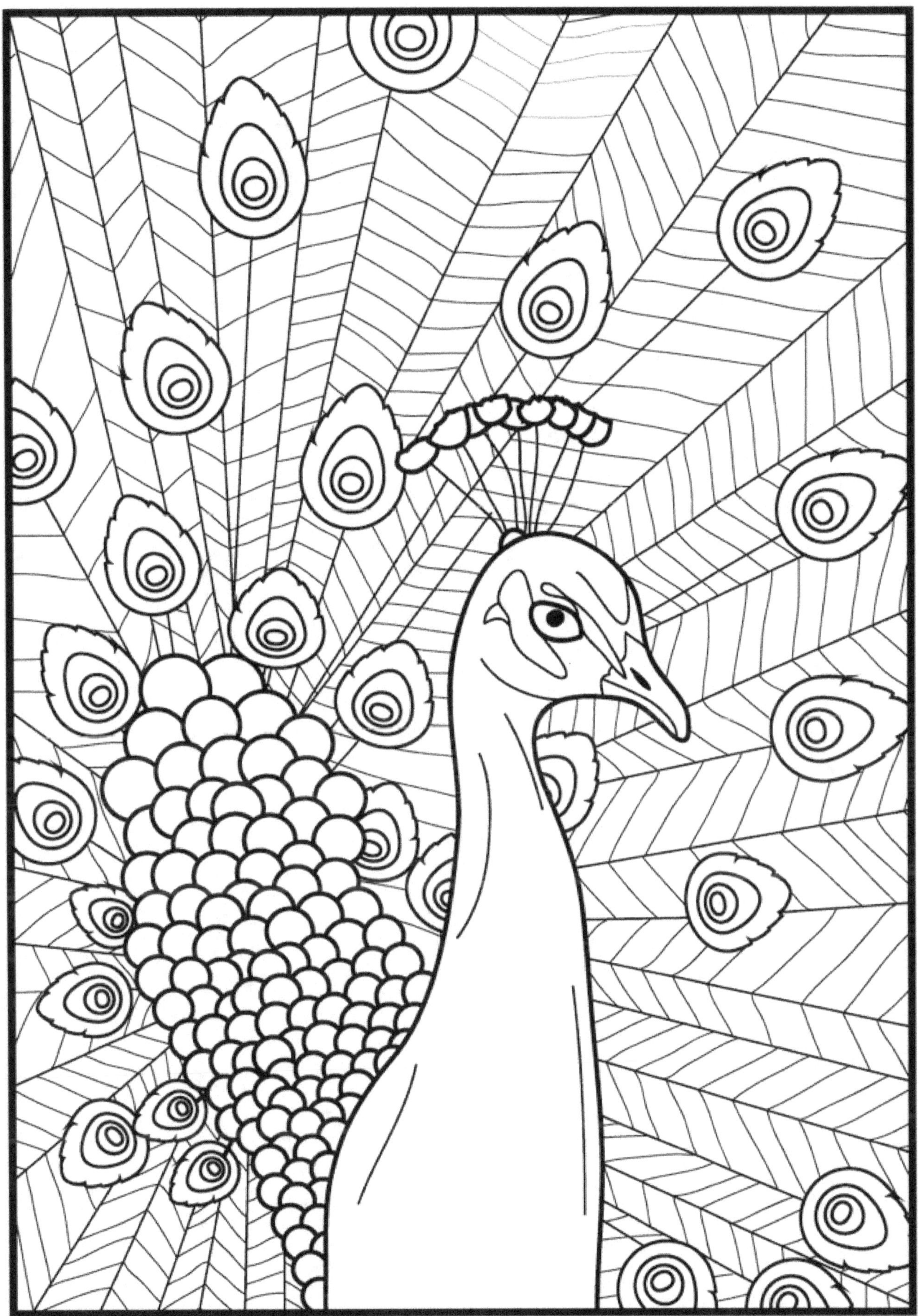

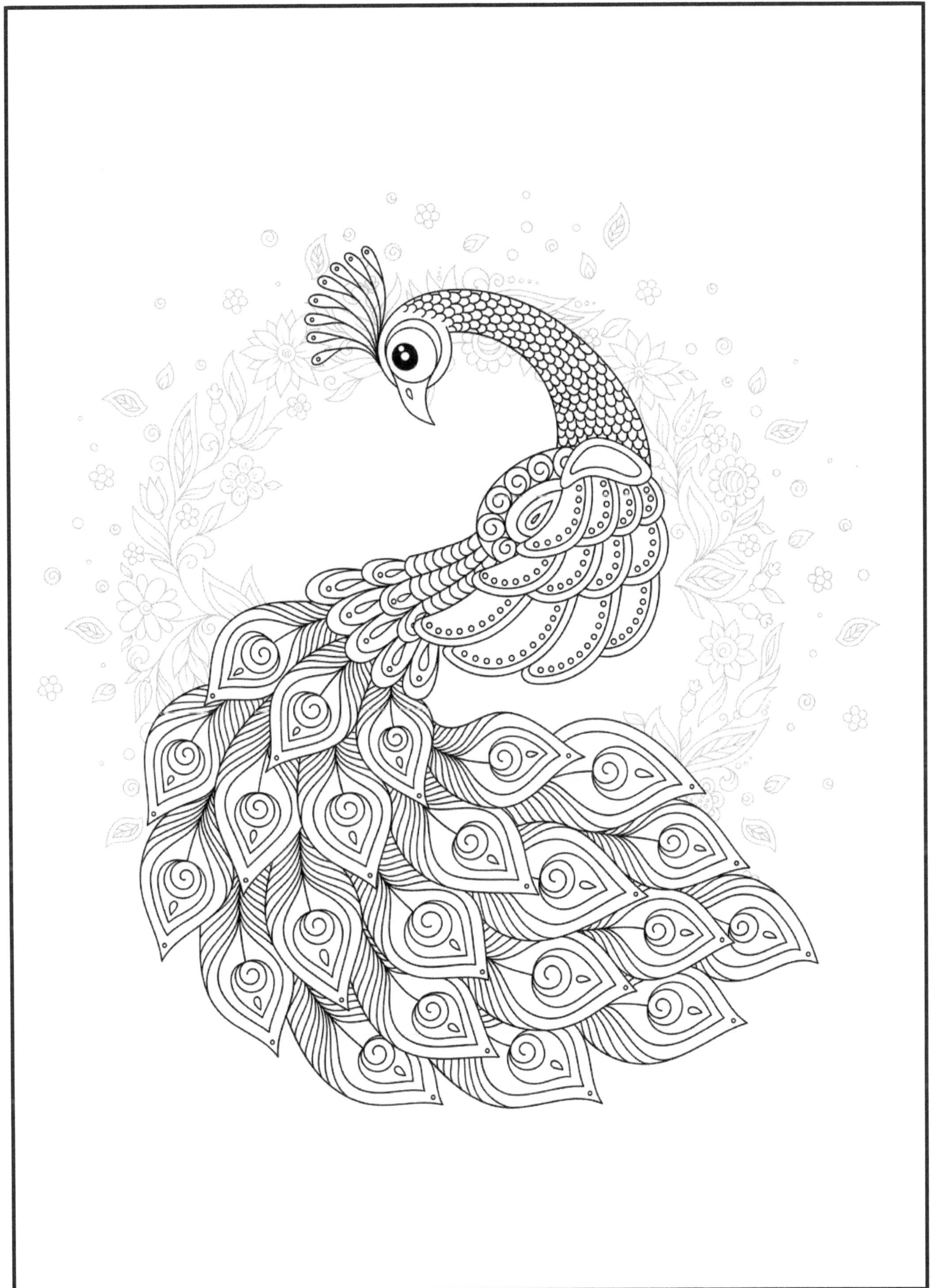

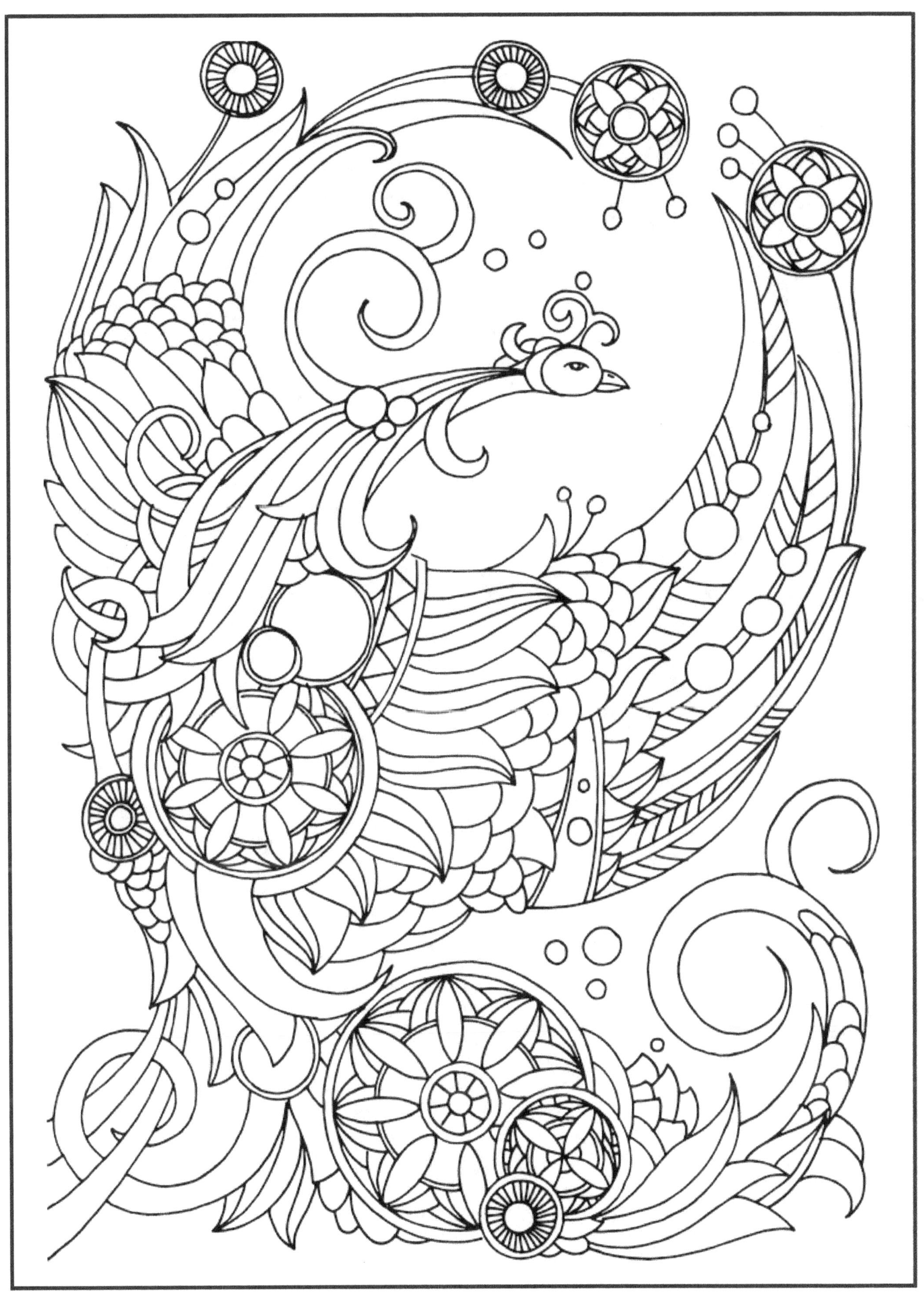

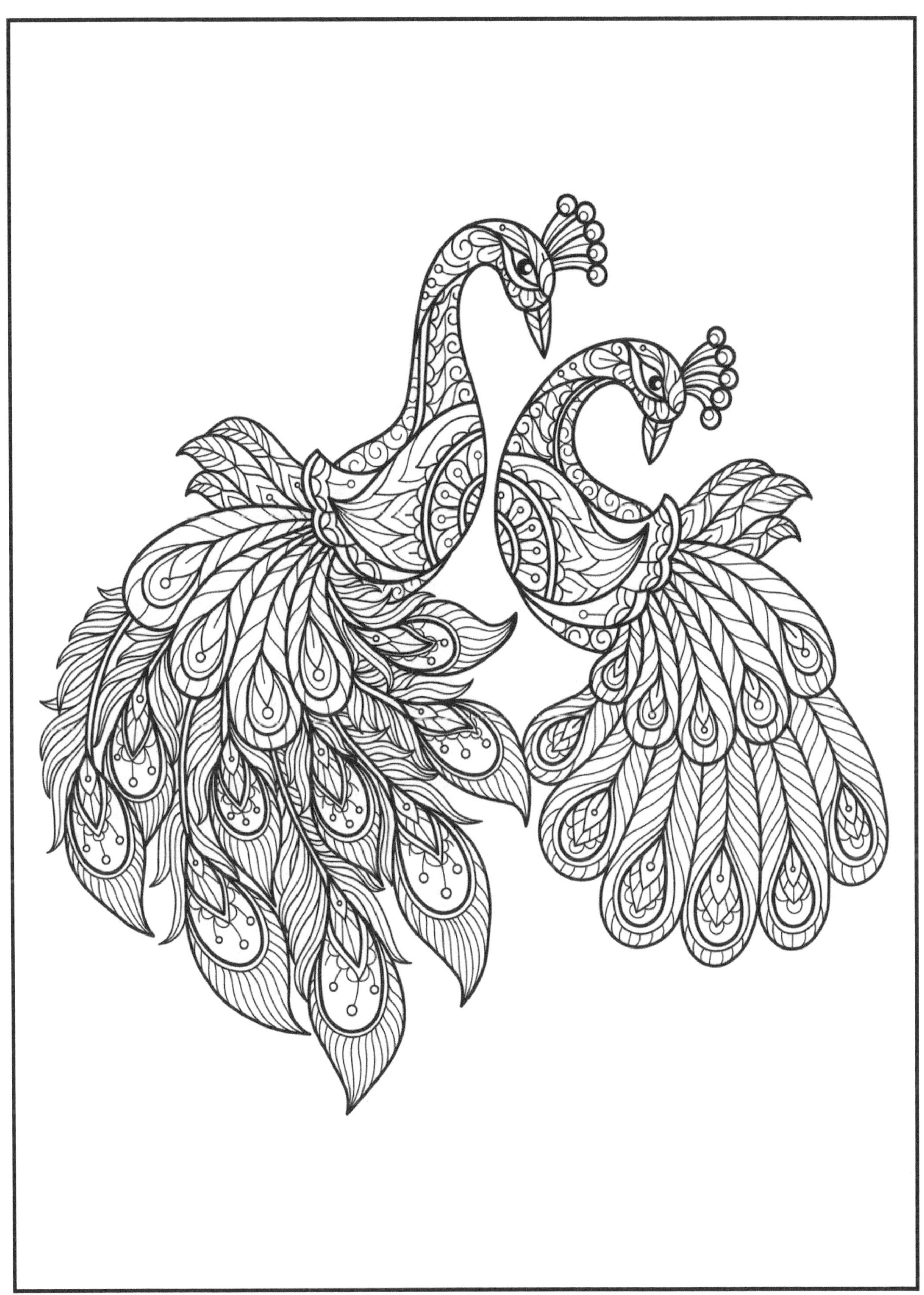

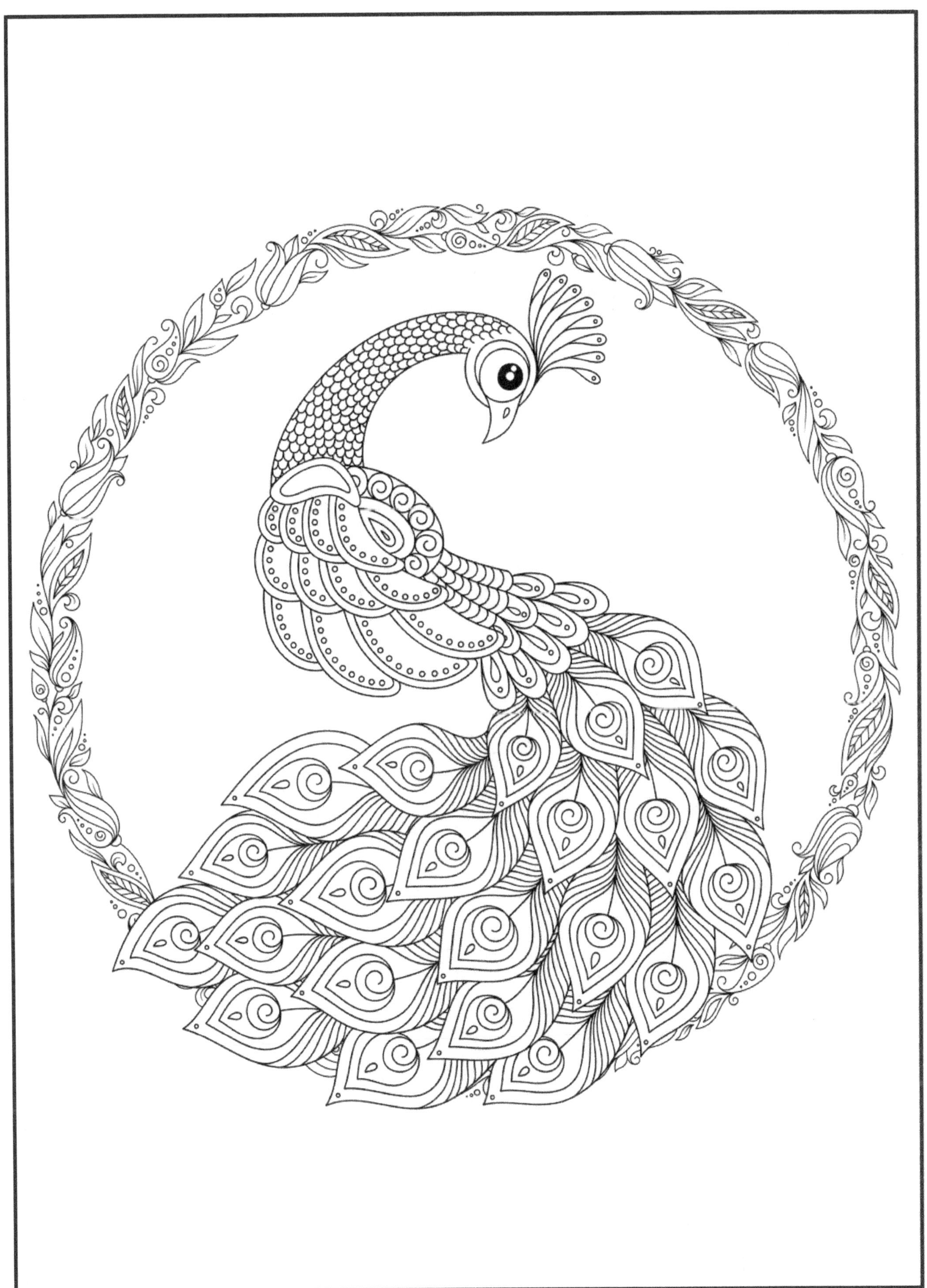

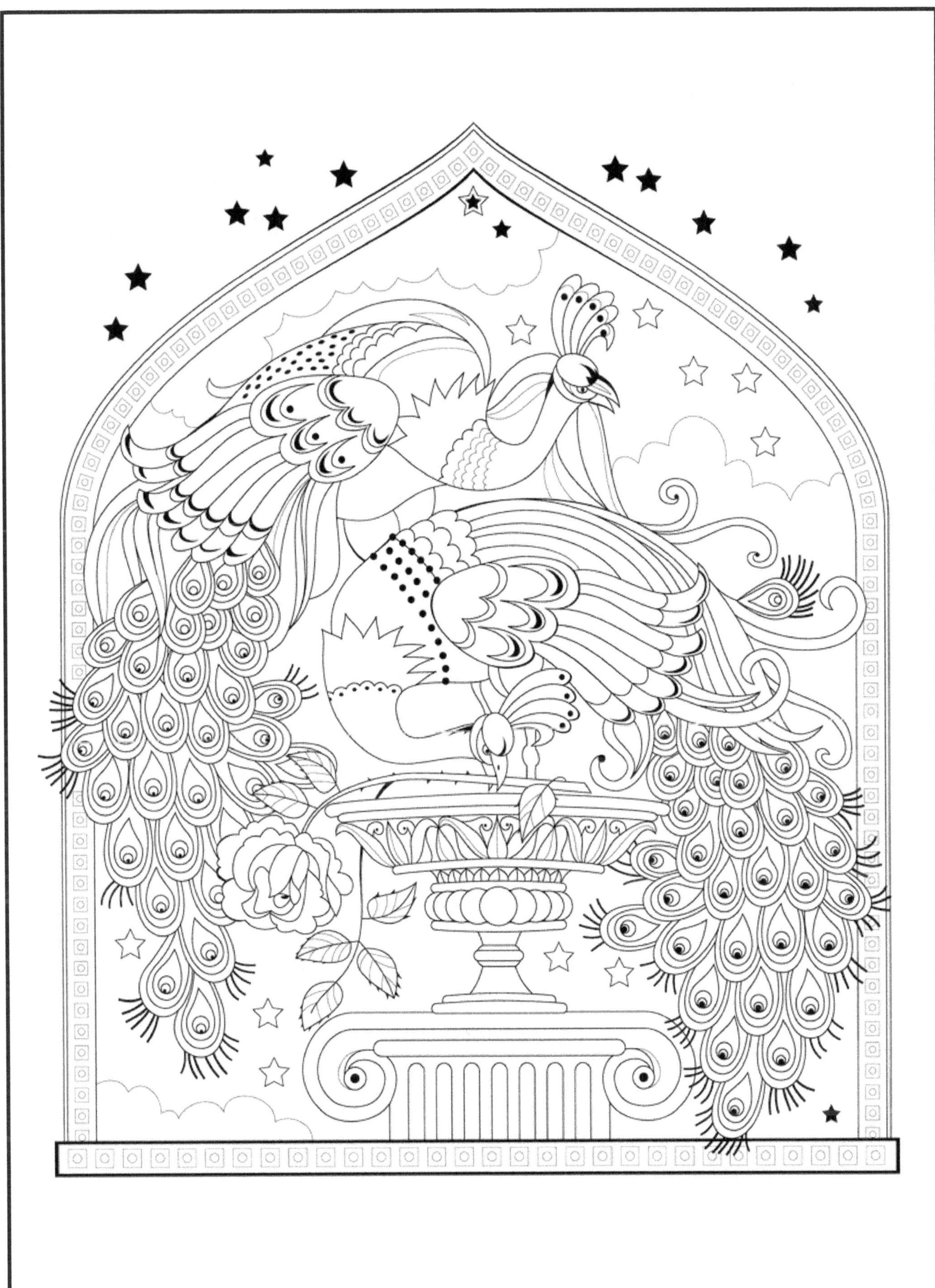

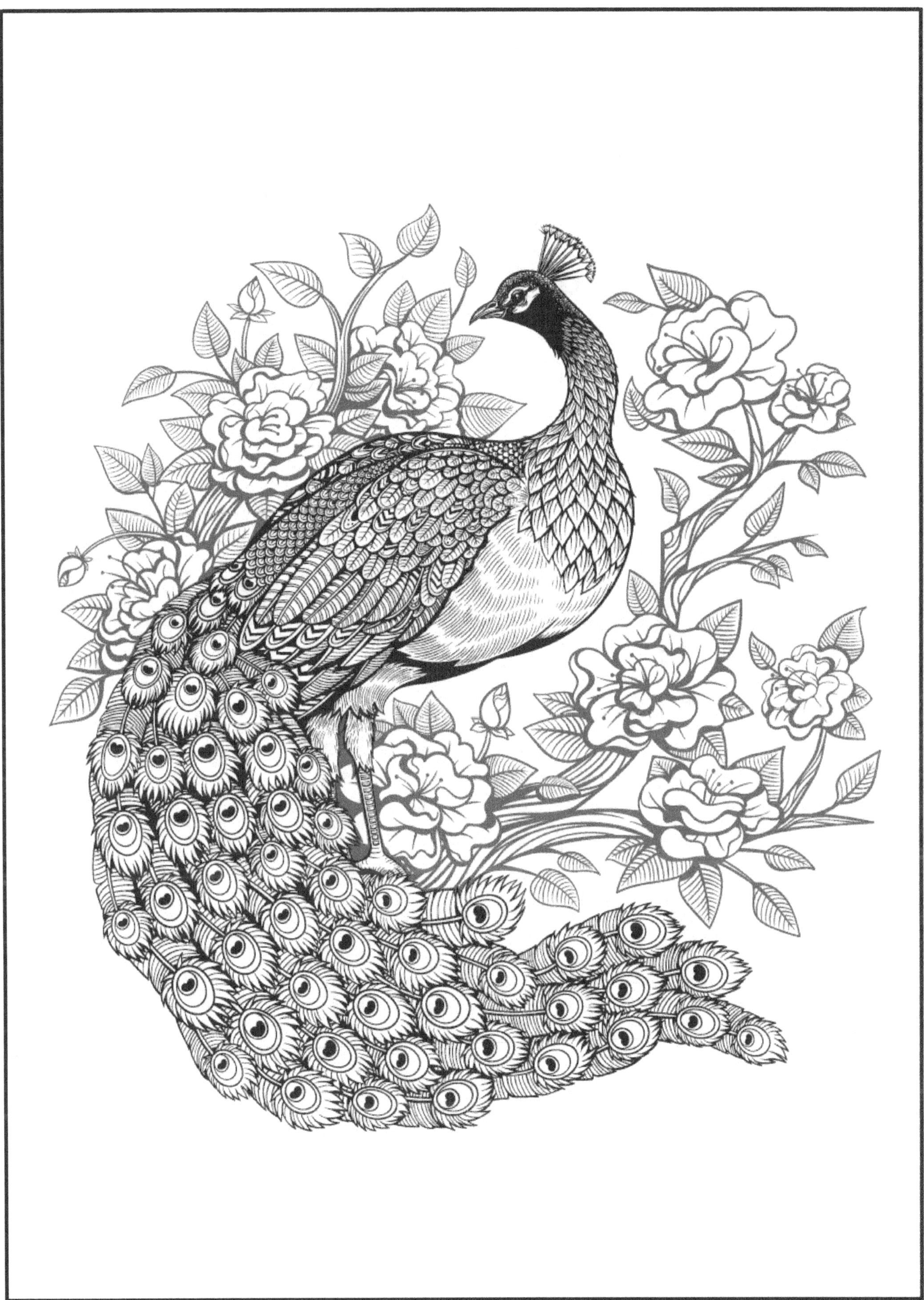

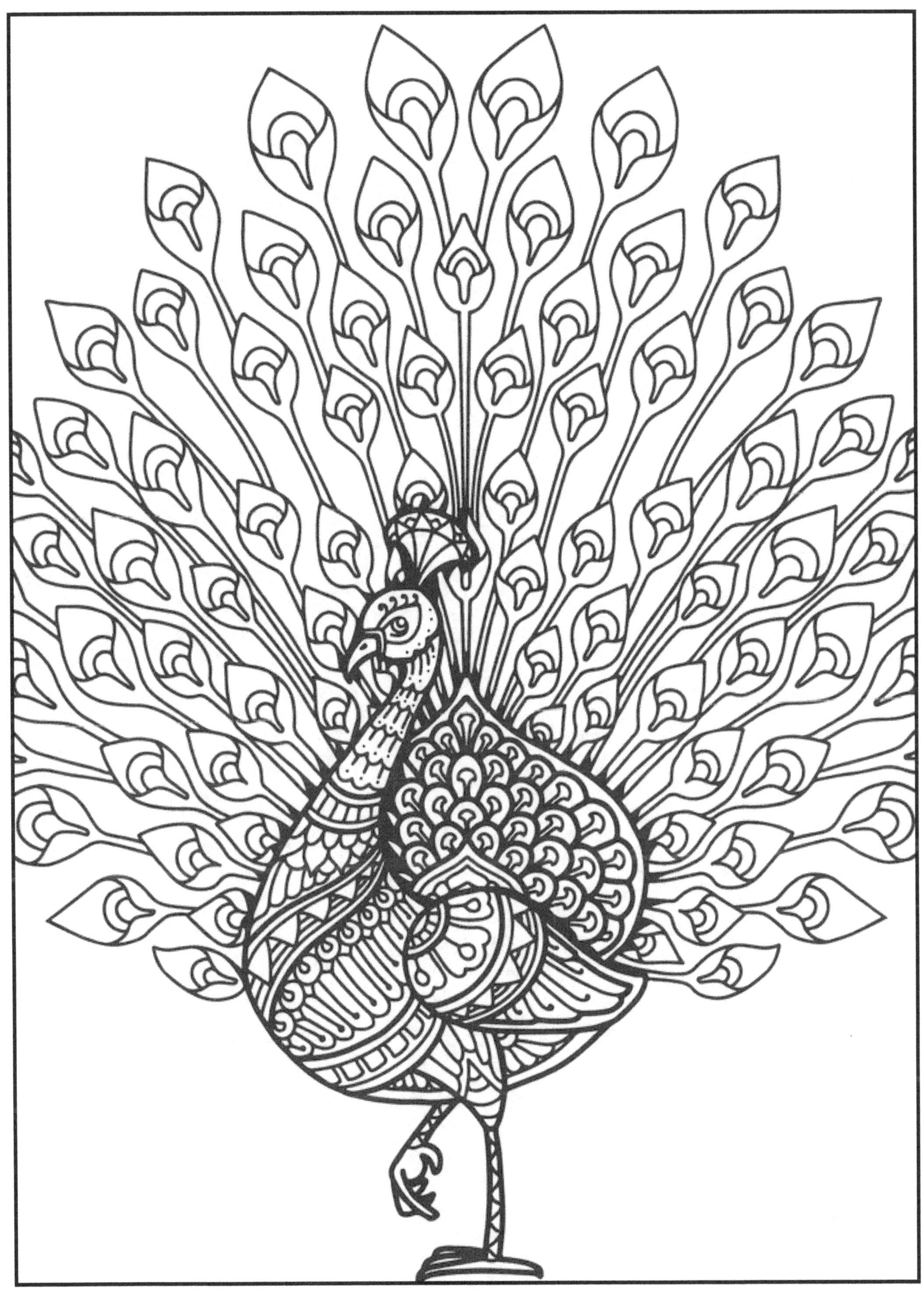

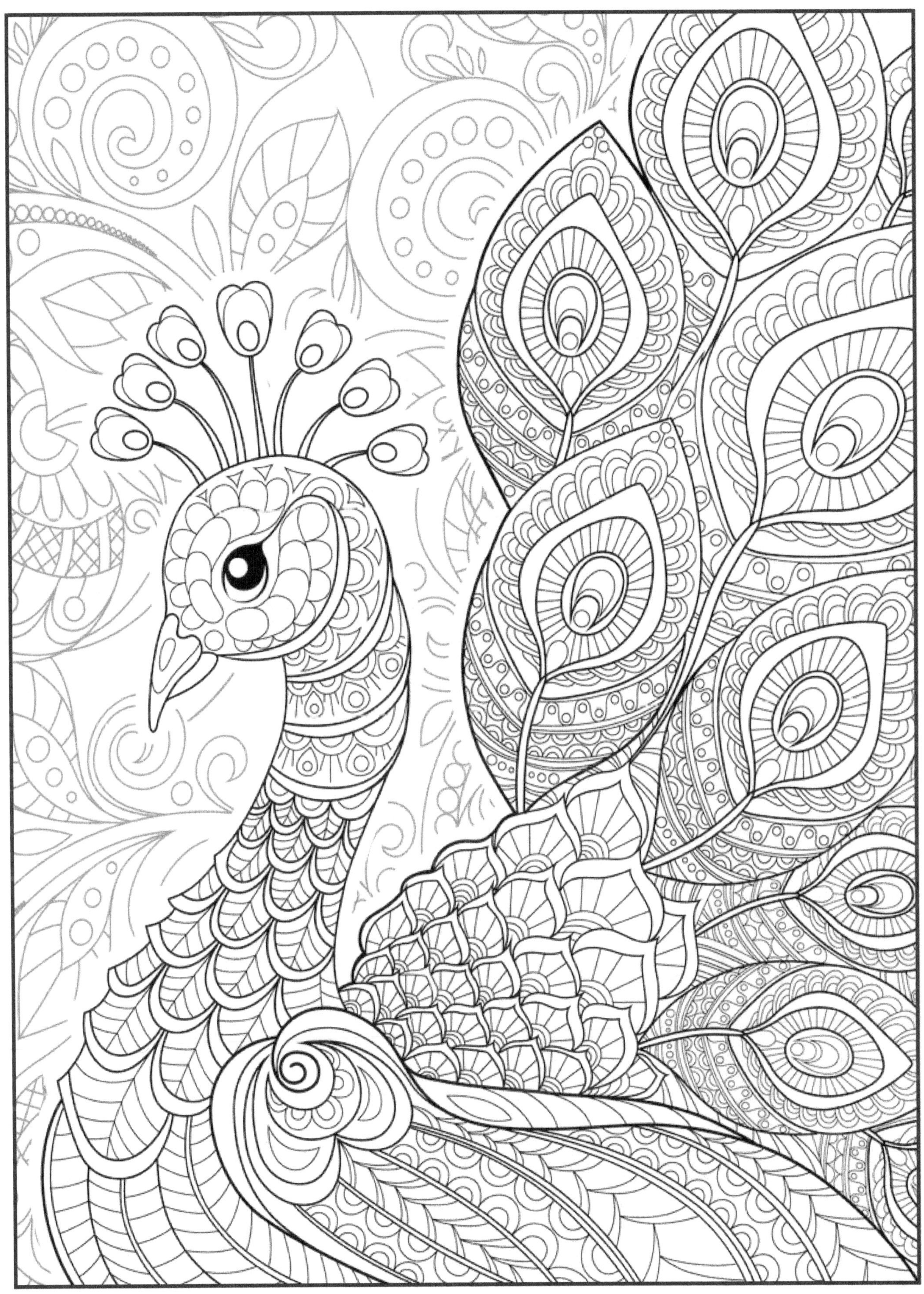

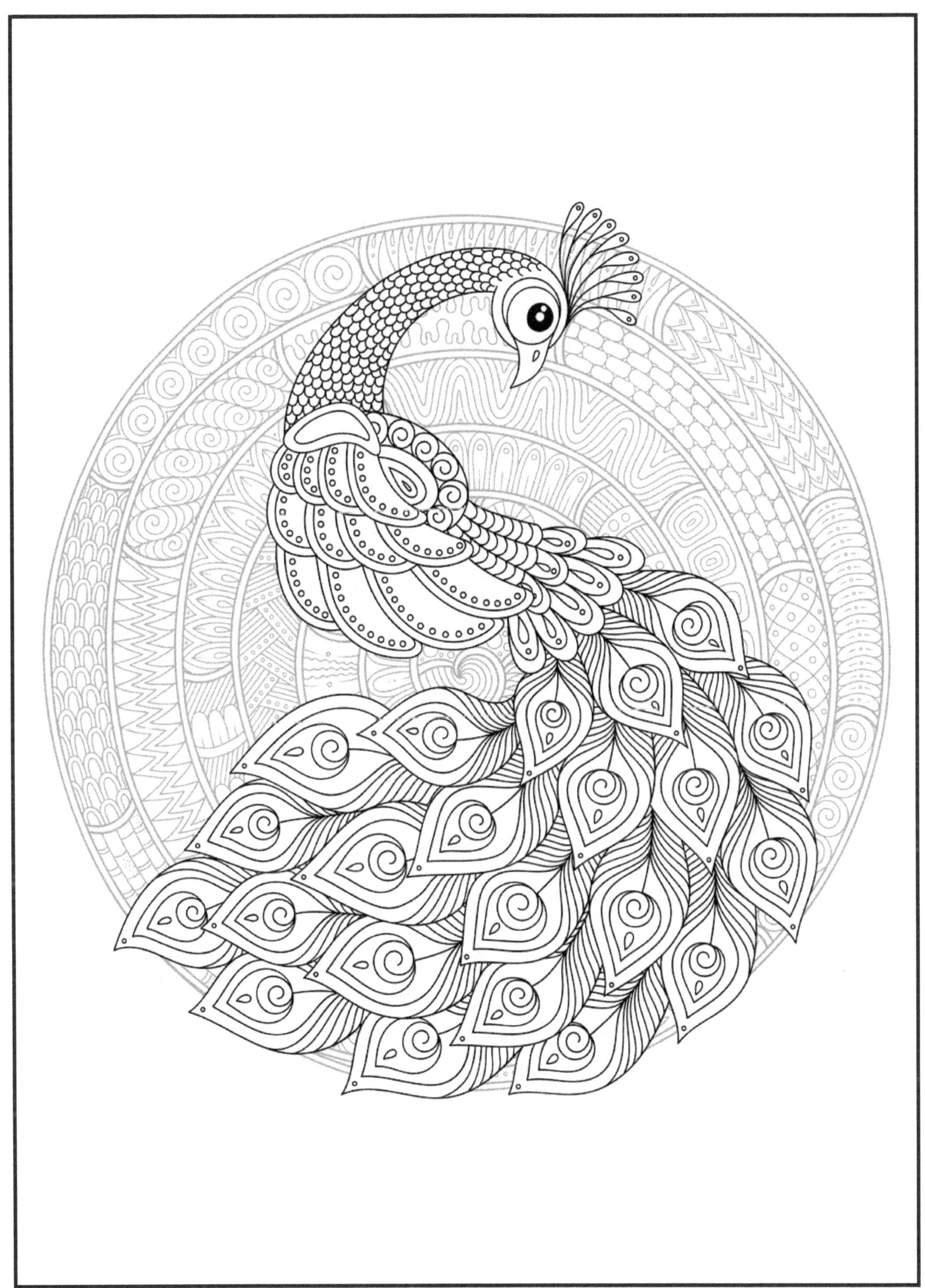

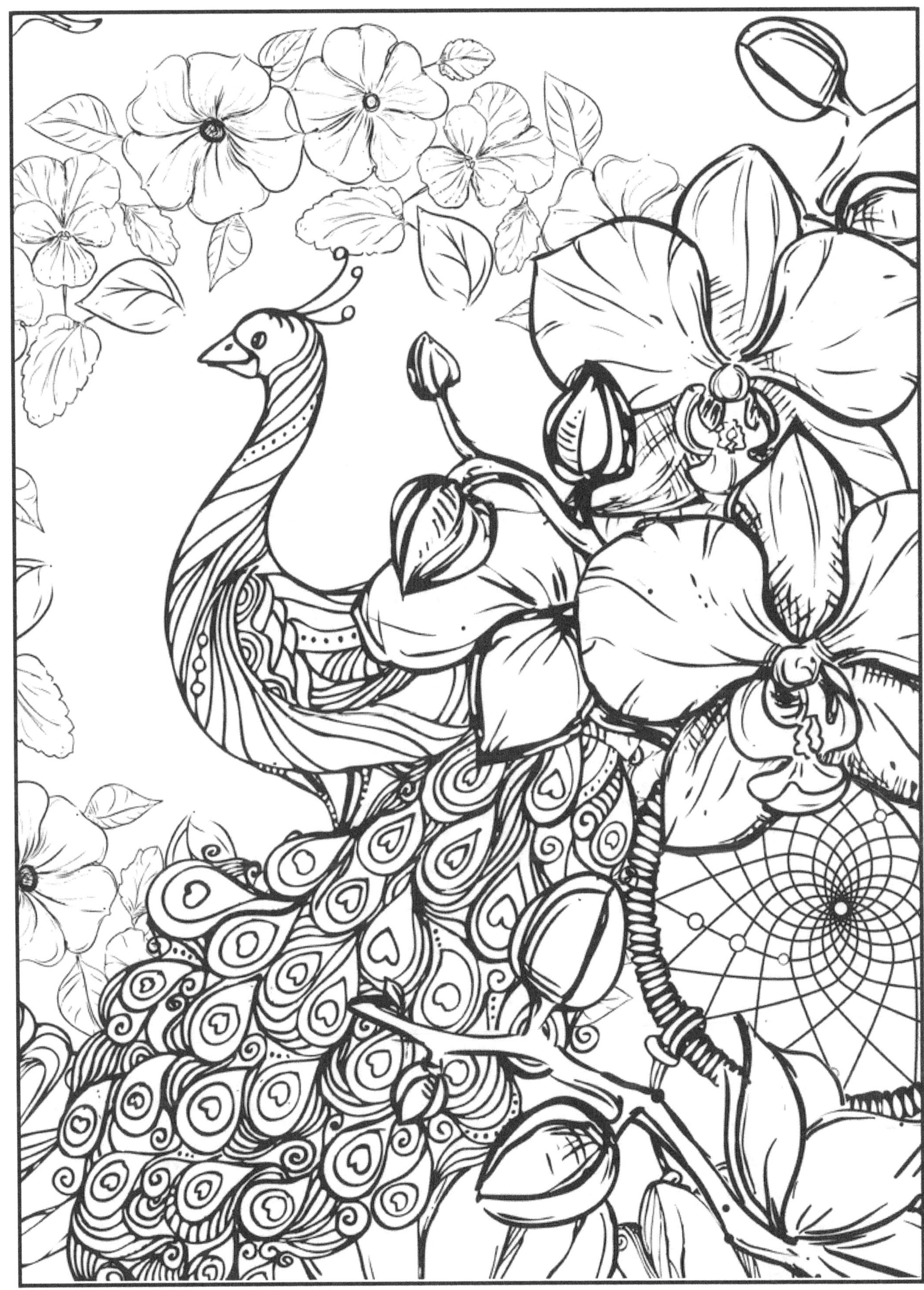

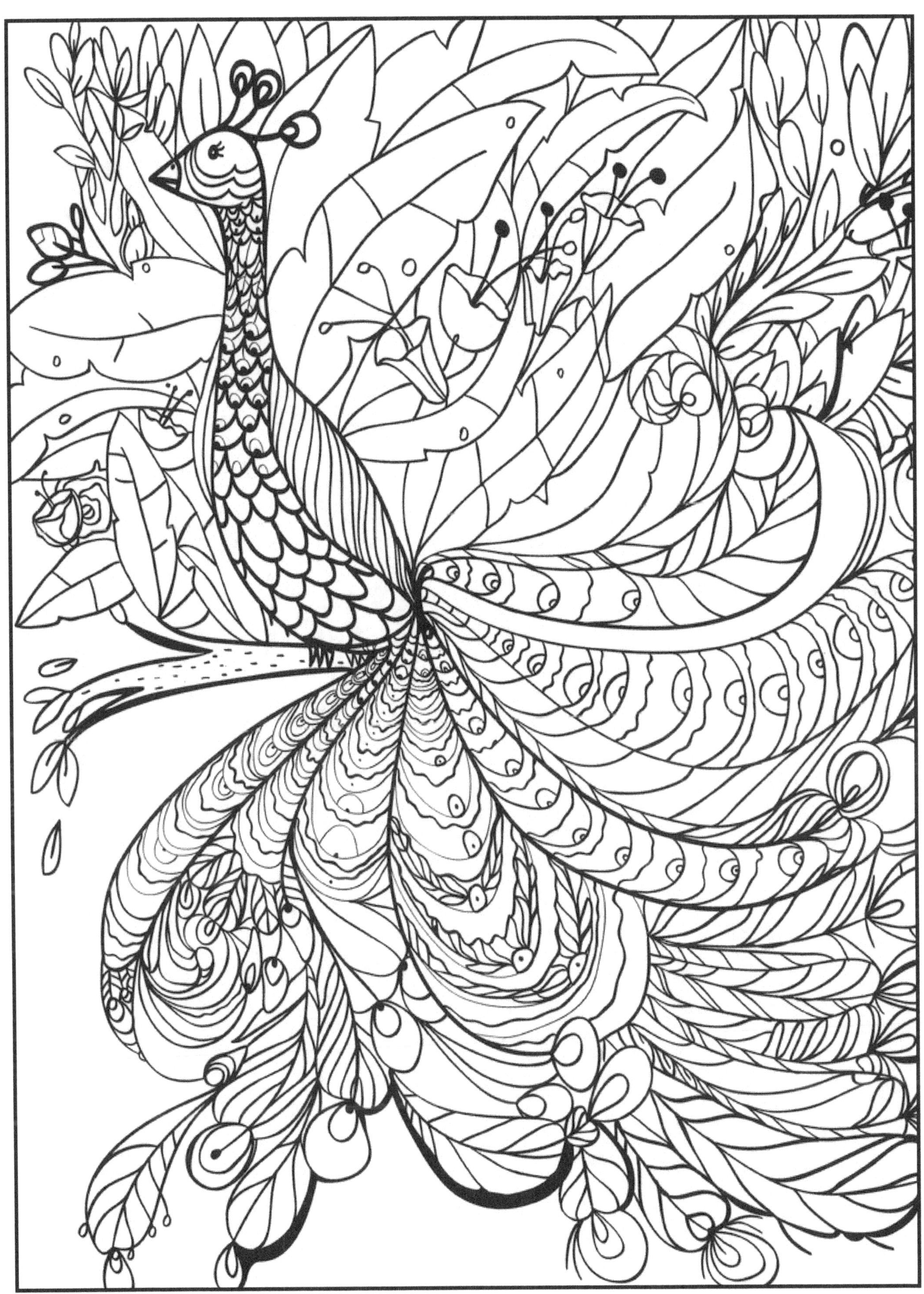

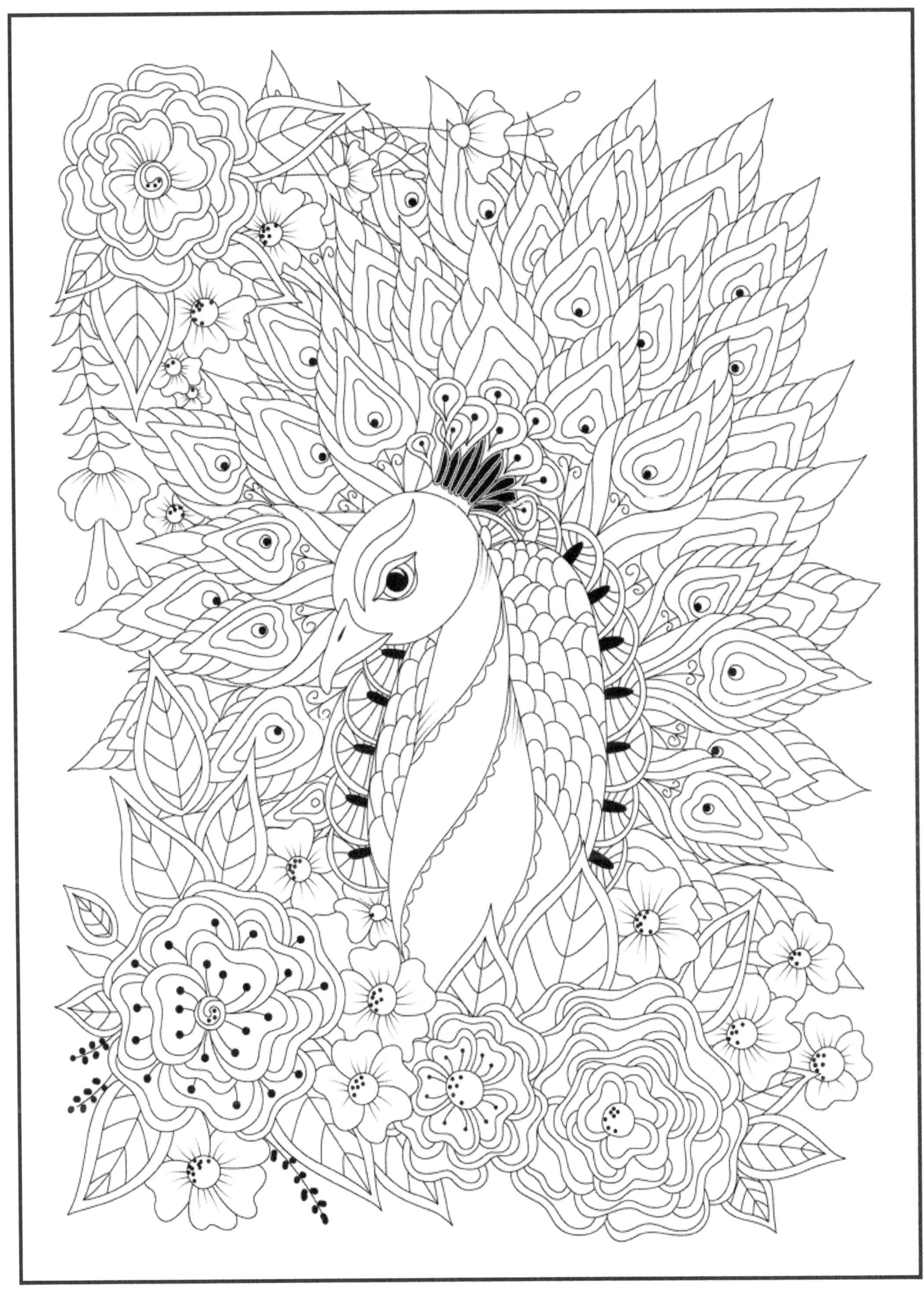

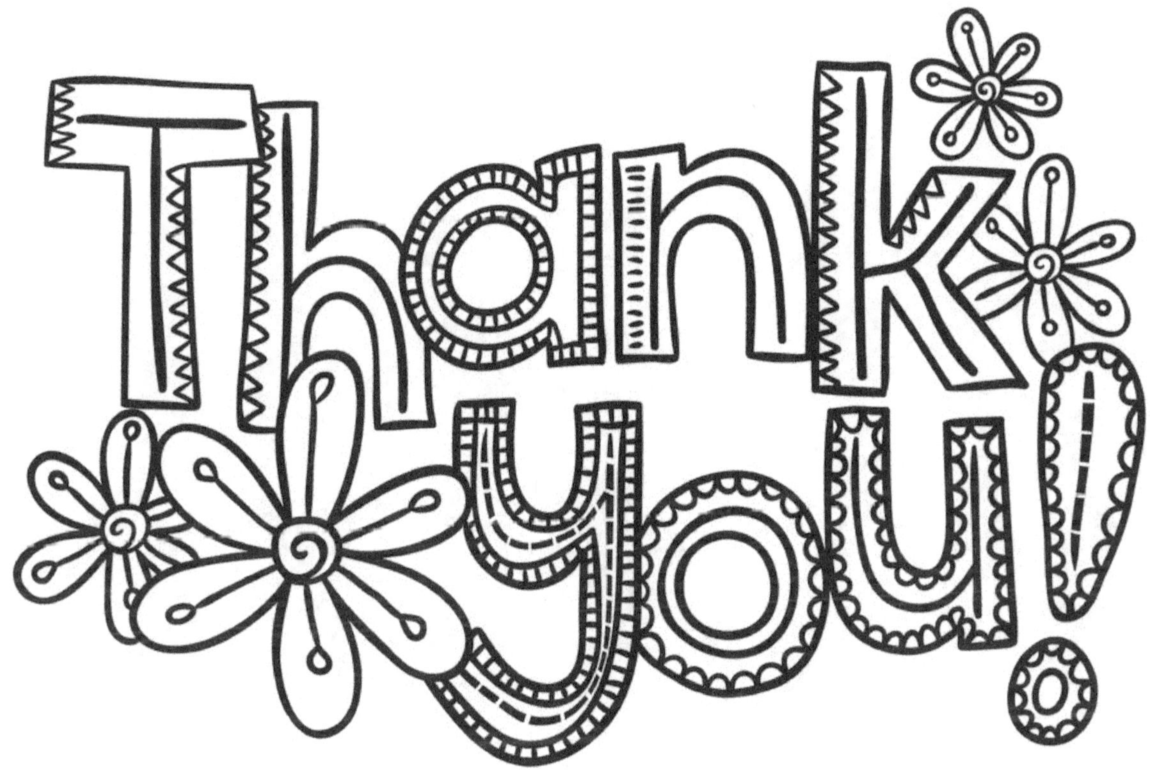
Thank you!